Grief Is Dark, But It Can Lighten II

When Major Life-Events Appear Impassable and the Pain Too Difficult

Jesse Montanya

© **Copyright 2024 - All rights reserved.**

The content contained within this book may not be reproduced, duplicated or transmitted without direct written permission from the author or the publisher.

Under no circumstances will any blame or legal responsibility be held against the publisher, or author, for any damages, reparation, or monetary loss due to the information contained within this book, either directly or indirectly.

Legal Notice:

This book is copyright protected. It is only for personal use. You cannot amend, distribute, sell, use, quote or paraphrase any part, or the content within this book, without the consent of the author or publisher.

Disclaimer Notice:

Please note the information contained within this document is for educational and entertainment purposes only. All effort has been executed to present accurate, up to date, reliable, complete information. No warranties of any kind are declared or implied. Readers acknowledge that the author is not engaged in the rendering of legal, financial, medical or professional advice. The content within this book has been derived from various sources. Please consult a licensed professional before attempting any techniques outlined in this book.

By reading this document, the reader agrees that under no circumstances is the author responsible for any losses, direct or indirect, that are incurred as a result of the use of the information contained within this document, including, but not limited to, errors, omissions, or inaccuracies.

Table of Contents

INTRODUCTION 1

SECTION 1: BASIC HUMAN COMPREHENSION 7

CHAPTER 1: YOUR BRAIN 9
   In This Chapter 9
   Understanding Your Brain 9
   The Brain: Fun Facts 10
   How the Brain and Mind Differ 11
   Why Is This Important? 13
   The Brain and Memory 14
   Brain Areas 15
   Why and How to Program Your "Computer" 16
   Retraining the Brain 18

CHAPTER 2: EMOTIONS, THOUGHTS, FEELINGS 21
   In This Chapter 21
   Emotional Awareness 21
   What Science Has to Say 23
   Cognitive DNA 24
   Grief and Memories 27

CHAPTER 3: THE CORRELATION 29
   In This Chapter 29
   Emotions, Needs, and Behavior 29
   The Emotional Loop 30
   Comparing Emotional Loops 33
   What This Means for Human Comprehension 35
   Grief Brain 36
   What's Next? 37

SECTION 2: MAJOR LIFE EVENTS 39

CHAPTER 4: ANXIETY—FRIEND AND FOE 41
   In This Chapter 41
   What Is Anxiety? 41
   Anxiety Is Your Friend 42
   Anxiety Is Your Foe 43
   The Biology of Anxiety 44
   The Psychology of Anxiety 45
   Anxiety Disorders 46

Seeking Help *52*
Samantha's Story.. *53*

CHAPTER 5: DEPRESSION—PANDEMIC PROPORTIONS.......................................55
In This Chapter.. *55*
Depression Is a Universal Problem *55*
What Is Depression?.. *56*
Types of Depression *58*
Getting Help *62*
My Depression Story... *64*

CHAPTER 6: DIVORCE AND ESTRANGEMENT 67
In This Chapter.. *67*
The Anguish of Divorce *67*
When You're Estranged *69*
Feeling Grief and Other Emotions *70*
What to Do *71*
Anne and John's Story *72*
Andrew's Story.. *75*

CHAPTER 7: POVERTY AND FINANCIAL HARDSHIP 79
In This Chapter.. *79*
The Problem of Poverty *79*
Basic Needs.. *81*
Finding Help... *83*
Turn Your Life Around... *86*
A Change in Mindset *88*
My Stories *89*
What's Next?... *91*

SECTION 3: CREATE POSITIVE CHANGE 93

CHAPTER 8: TECHNIQUES AND PSYCHOLOGY 95
In This Chapter.. *95*
Basic Psychology... *95*
Different Kinds of Grief *96*
When You Have a Problem *98*
Strategies That Can Help *99*
Cognitive Behavioral Therapy... *102*
Acceptance and Commitment Therapy *106*
Self-Talk *107*
Journaling *109*
Affirmations.. *109*
Art Therapy... *111*

CHAPTER 9: COMMIT, APPLY, REVIVE 113
In This Chapter.. *113*
Grief and Psychotherapy *113*
You and Your Therapist *114*

    Root Causes of Grief *116*
    Setbacks.. *117*
    Be Your Own Best Friend *120*
    Social Support... *122*
    Transforming Your Life *123*
    Moving Forward *125*
  CHAPTER 10: REDEFINED MIND—NEW LIFE DAWNS.. 129
    In This Chapter.. *129*
    Your Redefined Mind *129*
    The Story of Your Life... *130*
    Your New Life.. *131*
    Conquering Adversity... *132*
    Relish the Freedom *133*

CONCLUSION..**135**

REFERENCES **140**

Introduction

To anyone out there who's hurting, it's not a sign of weakness to ask for help. It's a sign of strength. –Barack Obama

I have been an Australian professional counselor for over 20 years. My skills were honed by the demographics of my clients. The first decade was spent mostly helping individuals, families, and communities cope with the most devastating drought this country has ever experienced and the emotions this evoked.

It was the first decade of the new millennium—a dark period for the primary producers of this country. The crops were decimated, livestock wiped out, and communities shattered, and this was happening year after year. The toll that the drought took was devastating for the people, but the anguish and heartache of facing the uncertain future continued after the drought broke. It was tough to be one of the people who had to face this turmoil and help the people suffering from it.

I conducted my work in the most remote outback regions of Australia. It wasn't typical counseling in which an individual would come to me for guidance with an issue. Often, doctors would ask me to go out and see someone in need. I received many phone calls most weeks. Most were from women who were distraught and desperate for someone to help their husbands and partners. I conducted my appointments in shearing sheds, out repairing fencing, in my truck at watering points, or checking on livestock. I would go wherever my client felt most comfortable.

The world typically pictures Australians as tough, hardened, resilient, and resourceful individuals. Often this identity is associated with farmers and other people who care for the land. "Toughen the fuck up" was a common saying these people used to get themselves through difficult times.

I had to develop a counseling style that was able to break through their attitude of simply not asking for help. Traditionally, Australians have had a certain isolation from people from other countries, and historically this has created a certain independence of thought and behavior. It was difficult to work within generational, ingrained belief systems that would never permit seeking counseling. It was just not in their character. But then, nature forced their hand.

My work has been multifaceted, involving one-on-one or group counseling, community development, courses and seminars, workshops, and guest speaking to promote mental health and prevent mental illness.

For 20 years, I have described my work like this: Professional counseling is a privilege when someone so desperately in need invites you into their life. They need you to address serious issues simply because they cannot. There is no greater privilege!

Now, I want to share my experiences and knowledge to help a greater population heal.

***

Have you ever just Google searched "What is grief?" "Am I experiencing grief?" or "How do I overcome grief?" If you are reading this book, there is a good chance you have. Searching for answers on the internet when you have a pain point such as grief is not likely to be very productive. Yes, there is information; the World Wide Web is fascinating and informative. The myriad of choices and resources can be mostly liberating if you are time-poor. However, when you are desperate for information, going through search results can be overwhelming.

The fact is that psychology is continually evolving; academic research and studies may conflict with or contradict information you find on the internet. However, don't be discouraged. Allow me to simplify matters for you.

So, what actually is grief?

In simple terms, grief is the natural emotional response to the loss of someone close to you. But grief can also occur after a serious illness; depression or anxiety; a divorce, separation, or estrangement; or other significant loss.

Grief often involves intense sadness and sometimes feelings of shock and numbness or even denial and anger.

Grief is a process or journey. It is not linear, and it affects everyone differently. Grief has no set pattern. It is expressed differently across different cultures.

Grief is complex!

Many people associate it with death. I have experienced a great deal of grief in my life, and it hasn't always been due to the death of a loved one. All that I write about in this three-book Grief Series, I have experienced personally and also professionally. I have counseled hundreds of people with the same experiences. Understanding their grief and my own has been the key!

I have found that people experiencing major life issues become overwhelmed with all the negative emotions involved. There is intense sadness, anger, shock, disbelief, and bargaining, which are all part of the complex emotional state of grief.

However, the difference is the involvement of other people and the circumstances associated with this grief. You may become consumed by anger, for instance, and focus too much on others' behavior. You may experience irrational thinking that is fueled by your anger. These feelings are difficult to resolve. If you group all these emotions as grief, then you have a framework to work from in therapy.

Grief is not linear; there are no timelines. Often, all the emotions associated with grief come flooding back in the therapeutic process. If you understand that this back-and-forth of emotions is typical, you stay engaged. That is the paradigm of grief described in this series.

Some may not associate grief in terms of anxiety and depression disorders or with divorce, separation, estrangement, financial hardship, or poverty. I would say 90% of my work has involved people with these major life issues. Often, they had endured years of trying to cope before they sought my help. With psychotherapy, my clients were able to learn how to alleviate their symptoms. Importantly, they were able to identify the root causes of their condition or situation.

Once you are open to identifying how you have arrived at this situation, grief can be expressed in your own time and frame of reference. You're able to understand your grief emotions, discover the link between thoughts and feelings, and, in turn, change your behavior. It is unforgettable when there is a release of negative emotion and anguish in your life.

This is a process, and it hurts. You need to commit to change. Life lessons learned can ensure negative emotions do not control you. In time, there will be emotional awareness that can aid you throughout your life.

My first book on grief focused on the process someone may go through when dealing with the death of a loved one. Many people can be overcome with grief and become lost. I allowed my readers to see what to expect and suggested what needed to happen to resolve their grief. With death, you need to feel the grief before you heal the grief.

This was a logical place to start: the death of a loved one as the first book in this series. If you have ever loved, you will experience grief due to the death of your friend, family member, or significant other. With the second book in this series, I'll talk about the grief experienced with major life issues. There is a difference in dealing with grief in these cases. There needs to be a commitment to the process toward positive change.

In this book, I explore the major life issues and explain the emotional responses that occur. I use professional stories and my own experiences to complement the content. I take a look at certain strategies and life-work that can bring about positive change in your current situation.

Remarkably, once you learn and apply these simple life lessons, you will never forget them. Then, as you journey on with your life and other serious matters arise, you can apply what you learn to ensure that you have rational thoughts, helpful feelings, and desired behaviors. This is emotional growth. You will essentially become your own therapist.

You will have created a positive new way to live life. Let me help you on this journey!

***

Note: Take a moment to reflect on the quotation that introduces each chapter. Think about the meaning it has for you.

All of the people featured in this book are identified by pseudonyms in order to preserve their privacy.

Section 1:

Basic Human Comprehension

Chapter 1:

Your Brain

Yesterday I was clever, so I wanted to change the world. Today I am wise, so I am changing myself. –Rumi

In This Chapter

The human brain is vastly more complex and powerful than the most sophisticated supercomputer ever built. Understanding how your mind works and the individuality created are the keys to unraveling the complexities you may encounter.

Understanding Your Brain

There's an awesome supercomputer above your shoulders. No, it's not a microchip that's been inserted there to further a billionaire's sinister plot. It's your brain!

All by itself, the brain is where thoughts and emotions live. It controls your body and all its processes. For example, the messages it sends to your heart and lungs keep your pulse and breath going. It regulates neurotransmitters and chemical actions and controls your hormones. It does all this without you having to think about it. In effect, your brain puts your body on cruise control. Basically, you can't live without a brain.

In addition to the functions that your brain performs without your conscious control, it also sends signals that you can choose to act on. Think about the simple action of picking up a cup of coffee. Your brain directs your eyes to focus on the cup. It causes you to reach out toward the cup. Then, your brain subconsciously informs your muscles to contract so that you grasp the handle and lift the cup to your lips. Your brain processes the information that the coffee is too hot to drink. It chooses whether you will blow on the coffee or add cream to cool it down. Then, it activates your swallow reflex so you can drink. The brain is involved every step of the way.

Consider your brain as a highly sophisticated computer algorithm. Every snippet of information, any stimulus at all, enters the database and combines instantly with all the other bits and pieces stored in your brain to bring about another snippet of comprehension. This may affirm or conflict with what is already in there; regardless, it adds to your individual programming. You instantly dial into this database when you consciously have a thought. If need be, you can tweak the database to account for new information.

You don't realize all the things the brain does for you because it operates for a large part without conscious thought. But, of course, the brain is where your consciousness lives and where thoughts arise.

You remember that you've used the last of the coffee and need to buy more. You wonder whether you need a new coffee maker. You plan to stop at the store on your way home from work. All these messages and thoughts are made up of connections in the brain.

Electrical impulses travel to areas throughout your brain that control language, thought, and action. And it does all that while keeping your heart, lungs, stomach, liver, kidneys, and other organs operating as they should. Your brain is the ultimate multitasker.

The Brain: Fun Facts

Now, let's have some fun facts about the most sophisticated supercomputer ever.

The human brain contains more than 100 billion neurons and over 100 trillion synaptic connections. In fact, there are more neurons in a single human brain than there are stars in the Milky Way galaxy (Yale School of Medicine, n.d.). There are approximately 100,000 miles of blood vessels that nourish this organ That's the equivalent of traveling more than four times around Earth's equator (Piedmont, n.d.).

Because of the fantastic number of neurons and synapses in the brain, its storage capacity is virtually unlimited. Information travels through it at more than 250 miles per hour. You may have heard that you use only 10% of your brain, but that's simply not true! The whole brain is involved in thinking, even when you're asleep.

You often see a light bulb above a person's head to symbolize thought. That's actually a good metaphor, as the brain generates enough electricity to power a light bulb (Piedmont, n.d.).

Even with all that going on inside your skull, the organ weighs only around three pounds and has a jelly-like texture because it's mostly made of fat. Your brain produces six different kinds of neurotransmitter chemicals that are responsible for muscle contractions, visual activity, sleep, body temperature, mood, and mental health (National Institutes of Neurological Disorders and Stroke, n.d.).

How the Brain and Mind Differ

The human brain has always fascinated me. Besides the chromosomes and genes that form your DNA, the foundation of your individuality is the stimuli you unconsciously and consciously put into your mind.

But what about your mind? Isn't that the same thing as your brain? Strangely, the answer is no. The brain is the organ that controls your bodily processes and actions. It controls most of your body's organs. It's the vital part of your central nervous system that serves as the hub for gathering, organizing, and disseminating information throughout your body. It's responsible for keeping your body going and storing memories as electrical impulses in different regions of its complex circuitry. It can retrieve those memories when you call on it to do that. But it doesn't determine what you do about them.

The brain has a specific location—in the human body, inside the skull. It's a physical thing. It's responsible for the physical functions of the body in one way or another, through stimulating the production of hormones or sending electrical signals through the central nervous system to the muscles and organs. You seldom notice what the brain does; it just automatically does all its jobs. Even when you consciously decide to raise your hand and wave at a friend, it's your brain that takes care of causing the muscles to contract and do that.

The mind, on the other hand, is the seat of thought and consciousness. It's what makes you aware of what's going on around you. It's responsible for what you think and what makes you, as a person, different from everyone else.

Your mind has three layers: the conscious, the subconscious, and the unconscious. The conscious layer consists of your immediate thoughts, feelings, and memories. The subconscious contains memories and behaviors that you have acquired over time. The unconscious is responsible for basic and primordial impulses such as the emotions of fear and anger. It's like a computer, too—what's put into it determines what comes out. If you put in pleasant experiences, what it returns is happiness and satisfaction. If you feed it bitterness and pain, what you get back is misery.

Your mind has different jobs from the brain, such as determining your morality, beliefs, reasoning, and understanding. The physical brain takes in information and stores it for retrieval, whereas the mind is intangible. It can't be seen or touched the way the brain can be. You can change your mind, in the ordinary sense of having a new opinion. But you can also change your mind in the sense of learning new skills. You can make new decisions and solve problems in different ways. Creativity and communication are controlled by the mind. Your brain may store what you learn about painting or needlepoint and control the movements of your hands as you practice, but the mind is responsible for the inspiration for what you create.

During your life journey, from infancy to where you are now, a great deal of information and stimuli will be stored away in your unconscious memory bank: things that are good or bad, threatening or pleasurable. You store away the information that forms your intellect—an understanding of yourself and the world you experience. From birth, your thoughts and emotions are continually refined like this. Every experience, every stimulus redefines your cognitive DNA, so to speak. Individual reasoning continually evolves, encompassing both the good and bad. You do this unconsciously.

Then, you can draw on that information and those stimuli to fill your brain with conscious thoughts. The different functions of the brain and mind work together to create the complete *you*, the sum total of your personality. Both the brain and mind are essential. You couldn't get by without both of them.

Why Is This Important?

You'll take quite a lot for granted as you continue forging ahead with whatever means you have to experience life. There will be moments in life when major challenges will affect your status quo. You may not be aware of how you got into a situation or how to recover the way you used to live. It's not until some adversity occurs during your life experience that you may need some sort of intervention to navigate forward. When you encounter major adversity in your life, you may need a little "brain work" to unravel the complexities.

Basically, you need to know what makes you tick before you can fix the clock. When something goes wrong with your brain, there are specialists such as neurosurgeons who can help. When you're experiencing adversity, such as a mental disorder, divorce, or estrangement, you may need to find out how you have gotten yourself into the situation. You also need to determine how and when normality can return. That takes a different sort of help.

You have many sources of support when you face adversity. Your family members can be extremely helpful in realigning your thoughts and feelings. So can close friends. The support they offer gives you a break from your confusion and pain. But when you wake up the next morning, the things that made you feel fearful or unhappy will still be there.

Often, you may need professional help. You should never dismiss the idea of seeking help for your problems. Your mental health can be fragile, and mental illness is serious. Getting help is not a sign of weakness. Reaching out is a sign of strength—you know enough about your feelings and thought processes to realize that you can't face this adversity alone.

When you share your experiences with a mental health professional, you are taking a step toward healing. They can help you understand what you're feeling and what you need to do to get back on an even keel. To continue the earlier metaphor, a counselor or therapist is an expert trained in clock-making and repair. They know how people tick and have techniques they can share that will help you face adversity and learn from it. You won't regret going for professional help, but you could easily regret not doing so.

There are professionals who specialize in managing different kinds of adversity, and you can choose someone who best meets your needs. If you're experiencing the aftermath of a messy divorce, for example, you could choose a therapist who works in the field of couples counseling. If you're reacting to childhood trauma, you may want to see a counselor who's well-versed in family therapy or inner-child work. There are even therapists who specialize in grief work.

The Brain and Memory

Memories are born in a region deep inside the brain. They can be classified into short-term and long-term based on how long they're stored. Short-term memories are fleeting—they come and go. Your short-term memory stores information that's not particularly important, such as the fact that you need to bring potato salad to the company picnic. There's no need to remember that past the date of the event, so it never makes it into long-term memory. You store information that you will need to use later in your long-term memory. The route from your home to your worksite, for example, is important information that you use almost every day.

Memories move from short-term to long-term when you use them often. The first few times you give a presentation, you need notes in order to remember the most important points. By the time you've given that presentation for the tenth time, you'll barely need to refer to your notes. The information has moved from short-term to long-term memory.

Other memories are even more deeply ingrained. You may not have been to your old neighborhood in decades, but you can still remember the route from your old house to the elementary school you went to and the playground where you met your friends.

Memories form based on electrical signals that pass from neuron to neuron within the brain. The signals encode information—emotions, thoughts, and feelings among them. When a memory pathway is reinforced by being used again and again, the signal is strengthened. If the signal paths are used often, the memory moves from short-term to long-term memory. Interestingly, many of these changes happen when you're asleep.

When you need those memories, your brain retrieves them from where they're stored and moves them into active use. You usually aren't even aware of the change. Like the route to work, the memory is just there when you need it. Different types of memories, such as sensory, motor, and emotional memories, are stored in different places in the brain, but they can all be accessed through neurons and synapses.

"Triggers" can also cause memories to surface. These triggers can be activated by sensory input such as sights and smells. In fact, smell is one of the strongest triggers of memory. If a man smells a certain brand of perfume, for example, it can conjure up instant memories of his first girlfriend. He doesn't know what the perfume is called, but he can remember the woman's name—even if he can't remember the names of other classmates from the time of the relationship—and the emotions associated with his memories.

Brain Areas

The different parts and functions of your brain are intimately involved in the emotions and thoughts you experience on your grief journey. The amygdala and the hippocampus are structures in the organ that help you process and store emotional memories related to grief. They make up what is known as the limbic system. Because it is involved in both emotions and memories, this system plays an exceptionally important role in grieving. The limbic system is also involved with the sense of smell, which may be why scents are such powerful memory triggers. The aroma of a spouse's favorite dish or the smell of their favorite flower can bring up memories that add to the grief associated with divorce, for example.

Another brain structure called the cingulate cortex is also a significant part of how your emotions form since it is another part of the limbic system. It plays a part in executive function, which is the ability to solve problems and pay attention to stimuli. If you are experiencing difficulty remembering everyday actions you should perform or feel abstracted and at loose ends, your inhibited executive function may be responsible.

The brain's stress response systems release hormones and other chemicals that affect your health. This means that chronic or long-lasting grief can also have long-lasting adverse effects on your physical health as well as your mental health.

The prefrontal cortex is the part of the brain that is involved in decision-making and emotional regulation. Grief can affect this vital part of the brain, making you have difficulty with decisions and also affecting the choices you make while you're grieving.

The action of mirror neurons is a recent area of brain studies. The mirror neurons may be responsible for certain effects including compassion and empathy. They operate by allowing the brain to process actions that you and others take. If you take actions that indicate grief, such as crying or expressing anger, someone in your support system who sees you will better understand your emotions and have an easier time sympathizing with what you are feeling. This will help them help you through your grief-fueled emotions.

Why and How to Program Your "Computer"

Your computer-made-flesh is an awesome creation. With the brain to encode data such as the bodily sensations that accompany the effects of hormones flooding your system, for example, you create a vast storehouse of information to draw on as you navigate through life. With the mind to tap into your brain's data, you translate those electrical impulses into thoughts and feelings that are responsible for how you react and what actions you take based on stimuli.

Occasionally, the computer develops glitches. Your emotions don't always react like you want them to, or they run wild and out of control. Unhelpful feelings may take over and cause you to behave in ways that are counterproductive and interfere with your happiness. When that happens, it's time to step back, take a look around at what's happening both outside and inside you, and make some changes.

You may think that it's not possible to alter how you feel about the inputs you receive from your senses. But that's not true. In the next chapter, I'll take you through the complexity of your emotions, thoughts, and feelings and offer some suggestions on how to reprogram them.

It's important to keep in mind, though, that you are an individual. No one has the same brain you do. The experiences you have are personal and unique to you. Your perceptions and your reactions to them build up your personality and your emotional makeup. Even if another person is present when a stimulus occurs, they will have their own reactions to it and thoughts about it. Their "computer" doesn't have exactly the same wiring as yours does, and the data that they have fed it won't be the same. It's no surprise that what comes out will be different.

For example, you and your sister go to a circus and see a clown. You had a clown plush toy as a child and associate clowns with comfort and happiness. Your sister was frightened as a baby by the sudden appearance of a clown jack-in-the-box and thinks of clowns as frightening. When you both see the clown at the circus, you laugh and smile while your sister turns away and cries. There's no right or wrong reaction; they're different because of what your brain-computers have been fed and how your feelings differ.

Your sister doesn't have to go through the rest of her life being afraid of clowns or avoiding them. She can change the way she feels and reacts when there's one nearby. By reprogramming her feelings through a technique like desensitization (slow, gradual exposure to what she's afraid of), she can change her unpleasant reactions to clowns until she enjoys them as much as you do. She can tweak her internal database.

Retraining the Brain

The brain has an awesome ability to change itself. This phenomenon, called "neuroplasticity," means that the brain can strengthen or weaken the connections in it (the neurons and synapses) according to how often they're used. In fact, the brain is always changing in response to what happens to you and how you feel about it. This happens because the neurons in the brain make and break connections between the synapses that convey information throughout the organ. If more connections form, the sensation or thought is reinforced. If the connections wither away, what you are feeling or thinking is less likely to be stored in your memory and acted upon.

When you are caught in a chronic stressful situation, your brain reduces nerve growth and makes neural connections based on the traumatic events. The more this happens, the more lasting the effects are. When the circuits associated with grief are activated, memory is decreased, and fear is increased in order to deal with the situation. If it goes on too long, grief can negatively affect memory, decision-making, and information processing.

This is particularly true of trauma that happens when you are young. Children's brains are even more "plastic" than those of adults. More connections are made, strengthening the memories and feelings. These adverse childhood events can have effects on mental and physical health going into adulthood. However, the same mechanism works in adults. Neuroplasticity happens in the adult brain, too. New, positive, and supportive experiences can retrain the brain in ways that encourage healing. Your brain can renew itself throughout your life.

This ability of the brain to change and grow is one of your biggest strengths in life. You may not think you can control your brain—it seems to just do whatever it wants—but it is possible to consciously affect your emotions and thinking. The stimuli that you provide for your brain will make subtle changes in its neural connections. Over time, reinforcing those connections will create pathways that can last a long time. When you don't think about certain things or don't experience certain emotions, on the other hand, the connections will weaken.

The same process of reinforcing neural connections can help retrain the brain to more effective functioning as well. Some of the techniques and strategies that I'll be discussing in some of the later chapters, including journaling and therapy, will help feelings of safety and security to return. If you find that a particular stimulus such as a scent or the sound of a piece of music brings you feelings of calm and security, you need to notice it and give your brain more of what brings these positive feelings.

You can also retrain your brain by giving it different inputs to focus on. Suppose you're afraid of snakes. When you encounter a snake, you can acknowledge that fear but tell yourself that you're able to take steps to counter it. You might use techniques such as standing still and not moving or backing away slowly. If you do this, your brain will learn that you can take these actions instead of provoking a traumatic fear reaction.

Chapter 2:
Emotions, Thoughts, Feelings

Your worst enemy cannot hurt you as much as your own thoughts when you haven't mastered them. –Gautama Buddha

In This Chapter

Central to your individuality, your comprehension of life, and how you live are your emotions, thoughts, and feelings. Emotional awareness is gaining knowledge of how these aspects of self work together in a connected way. It's crucial for both self-development and emotional healing.

Emotional Awareness

Emotional awareness, also called emotional intelligence, is a big part of what makes us human and is crucial to understanding what makes us tick. You need to be able to identify your emotions and understand them in order to function as a human being who interacts with others. Understanding the other person's emotions can be important, too.

Being aware of your emotions is the first step toward understanding yourself as a human being. What are you feeling? What name can you give to it? Are your emotions something that can change, or are they set in stone? Can *you* change them? These questions are essential when it comes to understanding your emotions. When you're dealing with grief, emotional awareness is crucial due to the complexity of the emotions involved. You may think you are feeling sadness, but underneath that, there may be a layer of anger. Anger can look like fear, and vice versa.

Many people refer to emotional awareness as getting in touch with their emotions. It is that, but it is much more as well. It's the ability to process your emotions and change them if necessary. You do this by changing your perceptions and your attitude, which I'll discuss more in Chapter 7. Changing those perceptions and attitudes can change the way you think about yourself and your life.

Why is emotional awareness important? For one thing, you'll have a better understanding of and communication with other people. Being able to recognize and interpret your emotions can lead to less stress because you'll be able to notice negative emotional states and deal with them appropriately. It will therefore help with your overall well-being.

Your problem-solving will improve because awareness of your emotions will help you think clearly and make decisions that aren't based on fear or anger, for example. But, most of all, emotional awareness helps you handle challenging situations. There will be plenty of those during your grief journey, so it's best to prepare for them by understanding your emotions.

Along with emotional awareness comes emotional regulation, or the ability to manage intense or upsetting emotions. Later in this book, I'll introduce techniques that you can use to do this, like mindfulness and controlled breathing.

As we discussed, your thoughts are like programs in the human-computer that is your brain. They definitely can change when they are provided with the proper input. How do they relate to your emotions, though? And how can you provide the input that will change your thoughts?

That's what I mean by changing your attitudes and perceptions. I'll be touching on this idea throughout this book. One example of changing your perceptions is if you want to change your thoughts about injustice in the world. To do this, you can look at the times when humans have acted nobly and kindly. This will allow you to change your thoughts to include the idea that there is more than injustice in the world. There is also compassion.

The other component of your emotional life is your feelings. Questions to ask include: How are emotions different from thoughts? Is it possible to reprogram your feelings as well as your emotions and thoughts? The changes you make in your emotions and thoughts automatically change your feelings. To continue the example from the previous paragraph, realizing that there is some good in the world allows you to feel that you can make a difference by practicing compassion and kindness.

Now, I'll take a closer look at your emotions, thoughts, and feelings and continue exploring how they combine to make you an emotional, thoughtful, feeling human being.

What Science Has to Say

As with so many subjects that science deals with, your emotions, thoughts, and feelings are hotly debated. Viewpoints differ on which comes first, your emotions or your thoughts. The cognitive appraisal theory, pioneered by Richard Lazarus, says that thinking occurs first. To start, you experience a stimulus, something that your senses perceive. Next, you think about it, and finally, you have an emotion regarding it, as well as a physiological response such as a fight-or-flight reaction (UWA, n.d.).

On the other hand, Ethan Seow, a mental health theorist, states, "From neurological research, the sensory input always goes through the emotional centers of the brain before it reaches the frontal cortex ... one must realize it is actually physically impossible for thought to come before emotions" (Seow, 2018).

Other theories suggest different mechanisms. For example, you can investigate different parts of and structures in the brain. Your thoughts, as well as emotions and other functions, occur in the cerebral cortex. The brain structure called the amygdala specializes in processing the feelings of fear and anxiety and your bodily responses to them, such as sweating and a racing heartbeat.

One thing it's safe to say is that thought and emotion are intimately intertwined in some fashion.

There are six basic emotions that all human beings exhibit: sadness, happiness, fear, anger, surprise, and disgust. Some believe that trust and anticipation should also be on that list. Grief, jealousy, pride, love, and other emotions are less likely to be expressed in the same ways across cultures. These are considered complex emotions; they are combinations of the basic ones. Whatever the correct number, these emotions can be recognized mostly based on the facial expressions that a person shows, which seem to be consistent across persons and cultures.

All these competing theories can be fascinating yet perplexing for the average person. The complexity of human beings and the intricacies of our brain function require further study. It is crucial, however, to gain understanding and knowledge about how emotions, thoughts, and feelings intertwine to shape the human personality and influence our responses to the various stimuli we encounter daily. Equally important is gaining insight into how individuals respond to negative stimuli and finding ways to alter those perceptions and emotions.

Cognitive DNA

Together, your emotions, thoughts, and feelings form your cognitive DNA, or your makeup as a unique individual. Basically, your cognitive DNA is the sum total of what lives in your head.

I call it cognitive DNA because, just as your cellular DNA defines your physical makeup—your height, eye color, blood type, risk of certain health conditions and diseases, the size of your nose, and perhaps even your taste preferences and temperament—your cognitive DNA defines your personality, your reactions to stimuli, and what you think about the world around you, to name just a few aspects. It's the nonphysical equivalent of the genes and chromosomes that determine who you are. And it's crucial for determining what goes on inside your brain.

Here's a look at how emotions, thoughts, and feelings differ and how they combine to make you an integrated human being.

Emotions

What are emotions? They're a reaction to a stimulus. You see a tiny kitten and have a pleasant reaction. You see a shark fin cutting through the water, and you react with fear. Often, we use the words "emotions" and "feelings" interchangeably, but there are distinct differences between them. Emotions are physical reactions—biochemical responses to the stimuli you encounter. They're already programmed into your nervous system and work like instincts. Emotions are not conscious but instead reside in the unconscious mind.

Emotions impact our bodies on a physical level by affecting bodily systems such as blood flow, heart rate, sweating, and alertness. Emotional responses are therefore biologically based and instinctual. Some basic emotions are fear, anger, joy, and disgust. Certain experts believe that these emotions don't vary greatly between individuals, at least not in the general sense. The next chapter will expand on this idea.

When you experience trauma, you manifest heightened levels of anxiety (to be discussed further in Chapter 4). That anxiety will lead to persistent negative feelings and irrational thoughts and behavior. Life can quickly spiral into a troubled, unhappy, desperate state. Once your thoughts focus on the overwhelming emotion, you are then being controlled by that emotion rather than controlling it. You create a block between your mind and rational thought.

Yes, we manifest emotions in the unconscious mind, but let's see how thoughts and feelings determine who we are and how we are.

Thoughts

Thoughts are mental processes that link your emotions with your feelings through perception, interpretation, reasoning, and memory. All your experiences, including your beliefs, culture, desires, dislikes, and actions, make up your thoughts. You think and then you store what you've thought. I mentioned before how your mental database is continually being refined from the time of your birth to today. Every stimulus you experience creates an emotion and then a thought that is filed away in your mind. This is a large part of what makes you human.

Unlike your emotions, your thoughts can be conscious. Thoughts are useful for interpreting information and making decisions. A lot of the time, your thoughts are devoted to mundane tasks. You think about what you need at the grocery store or ask yourself if you're going to be late for work. But you also have deeper, more serious thoughts. You can think about your place in the world or how the universe came to be. You can think about whether there is life after death.

Feelings

Feelings are experienced consciously and physically. How you are feeling at any one moment is determined by your experiences, memories, or stimuli; your emotions; and your thoughts. For example, if you're thinking about your place in the universe, you may *feel* small and insignificant. If you're out of money, you can have *feelings* of frustration because your *emotions* about poverty are frightening, and your *thoughts* about your situation tell you that there's no clear way to resolve the situation. Your feelings are the result of the thoughts that are built up by your personal experiences, memories, and emotions.

All this happens in an instant, which is possibly the reason that experts hold contradictory opinions about what comes first, emotion or thought. The process I've described—first emotions, then thoughts, and then feelings—explains a lot of human behavior and guides your actions.

Without your cognitive DNA of emotions, thoughts, and feelings, you wouldn't be fully human. For lower-order animals, there is debate about whether they have emotions, thoughts, and feelings. It seems likely that they have thoughts. A cat may use its senses to determine where a mouse is and may have thoughts about how best to catch it—to stalk it or simply to pounce—based on its perception of whether the mouse is moving or stationary. The cat may experience a feeling of satisfaction after it eats the mouse, or perhaps it merely has the physiological perception of a full stomach. Certainly, they react to stimuli. But does the cat have what we would call emotions?

Their emotional range seems to be limited compared to ours. There's no doubt that a cat can feel the emotion of fear when it encounters an unfamiliar dog or anger when another cat steals its food. But joy? Cat owners will say cats do feel this when they're sitting in the sun or being petted. Others believe that these are simply physiological reactions to sensory input. The jury is still out.

For now, it's safe to say that cognitive DNA, the combination of emotions, thoughts, and feelings, is a vital component of human existence.

Grief and Memories

How does your mind make and store memories? And how do they change as you go through the process of grieving? As you might expect, your mind has a lot to do with it. While your brain actually encodes memories and stores them for retrieval, your mind is responsible for the emotional content and the connections between your memories and your emotions.

First, the grief for any kind of loss leads to memories that are highly emotionally charged. The memories that have that emotional resonance are more likely to be stored and more likely to be vividly recalled. Your memories may include flashbulb memories—very vivid and long-lasting ones—of when you heard the news of a traumatic event. But the emotions you experience during your grief journey have to be stored and interpreted. Your emotional state will determine which memories will be detailed or fragmented.

The emotional content of your memories can also be affected by grief. For example, you may vividly remember pleasant moments with your estranged children, but your recall of events could be selective: you might remember only the good times or only the bad. Your emotional state will determine which of those happens. Your emotions may affect the recall process, leaving you unable to access some memories or triggered by others.

Emotional triggers can be attached to memories. When you access a certain memory, you may be overwhelmed by the emotions you felt when that incident first happened. Memories that trigger you have a lot of power. Triggered memories can thrust you back into the past with a physical reaction or buried emotional state, causing you to relive the trauma. A memory trigger can cause a flashback or a meltdown, no matter whether you're in the privacy of your home or out in public. It's similar to what happens in post-traumatic stress disorder (PTSD).

Another possibility is that you will begin to ruminate, or obsess about, your memories. You could think about your loss over and over, leading to certain memories dominating your thoughts. Whether they are pleasant or unpleasant can shape how you view your loss and can affect your ability to work through your grief.

You have two different kinds of memory—emotional and factual. While you are grieving, the two may become intertwined. You can recall the facts of your loss, but the emotional content might overlay them. You might invest great emotional significance in a neutral memory, for example. This can affect how you recall incidents that led up to your loss.

Because your emotions and events are consolidated when you dream, what happens while you're asleep can alter your understanding of and reactions to your emotions and thoughts.

Basically, your memories can be adaptive, leading you to recall good times and pleasant emotions, or maladaptive, causing you more pain and grief. There's no predicting which it will be. Your memories and emotions are just another part of grief that you'll have to get through.

Chapter 3:
The Correlation

Self-awareness is probably the most important thing towards being a champion.
–Billie Jean King

In This Chapter

Your emotions, thoughts, and feelings not only determine your understanding of the world but are the foundation of your individuality. If you engage in self-discovery, understand how human beings develop, and comprehend your humanity, you will have the ability to overcome adversity.

Emotions, Needs, and Behavior

Emotions, feelings, and thoughts vary depending on the individual, but ultimately, they form the foundation of our human comprehension of the world and our responses to life. They're also what makes every human being unique. Who you are and what you do are determined by the interaction of emotions, thoughts, and feelings.

This interaction happens in specific ways, which I'll discuss in this chapter. This is very important regarding how you understand the world and yourself. When you discover the forces working inside you, understand how the human person develops, and comprehend your humanity, you will have the ability to overcome adversity.

Self-awareness is a goal of human development that not everyone achieves. Pioneering psychologist Abraham Maslow worked out a theory called the hierarchy of needs. These are the levels of human development that each person goes through.

The two lowest levels are considered basic needs. The first level is basic physiological needs for food, water, shelter, and warmth. Once you have achieved that level, you move up Maslow's hierarchy (or pyramid) to safety needs, which include both safety and security. These can entail having a job that helps you meet your personal or family obligations.

Next is the need for belonging or love. This can come from family or friends, intimate relationships, or being part of a meaningful group that feeds your need for human interaction. Above that on the pyramid is the need for esteem: a feeling of accomplishment and positive feedback. This group is called psychological needs.

Finally, the top layer can be reached if all the previous needs are met. This is called self-actualization or self-fulfillment. It can encompass creative achievements as well as achieving your full potential. A person who is self-actualized understands their needs, but more importantly, they understand their emotions, thoughts, and feelings. According to Maslow, few people ever reach that level. Most of us get stuck on one of the lower levels (McLeod, 2018).

Much of adversity happens when these needs are not met. Food, shelter, and safety needs can be compromised by poverty, financial hardship, and natural disasters, for example. Deficiencies in a sense of belonging or love can be triggered by abandonment, divorce, or estrangement. And you probably won't be able to achieve the satisfaction of high self-esteem or self-actualization if you suffer from anxiety or depression.

These are problems that I'll address in future chapters. For now, just know that emotional awareness is easy to comprehend in the abstract. Far more challenging is the way that it interacts with your human nature to produce behavior that you can use to cope with serious life issues.

The Emotional Loop

Your emotions, thoughts, and feelings make up a kind of loop. You have core beliefs about yourself, other people, and the world. Some of these beliefs might be whether you are a good person, other people are kind, or the world is fair. Or you might have core beliefs that say that you are flawed, other people are selfish, and the world is rigged against you. These beliefs, along with the situation you're confronting, combine with your emotions, thoughts, and feelings to create your behavior. Your behavior, in turn, causes you to have more emotions, thoughts, and feelings about the effects of your actions.

When you understand how these factors work together, you can use this emotional awareness to respond when major negative life issues occur, including assorted hardships.

Once outside stimuli result in emotions, your thoughts play a role in how you interpret and evaluate them. Your thoughts help you make sense of the way you feel—if you have emotional awareness. There exists a continuous feedback loop connecting emotions, thoughts, and feelings. Thoughts have the power to influence emotions and feelings, while emotions can shape thoughts and subsequent feelings. This dynamic interaction perpetuates an ongoing cycle.

Thoughts play a part in regulating and coping with emotions. Constructive thoughts, for example, can help manage emotions and behavior. If you have the emotion of fear when it comes to taking tests, for example, constructive thoughts might relate to the fact that you can influence what your grade will be. Those thoughts are then converted into behavior: You study for the test. This in turn affects your emotions, giving you more confidence and pride.

Your personal situation, such as your culture, your age, and your family of origin, makes a difference in your emotions and your emotional loop. A person from one family might have a stimulus of an upcoming dentist appointment and react to it with the emotion of fear. Someone who has had different, more positive experiences might have neutral emotions. This will determine what they think about going to the dentist. For example, "I hate this!" or "I always do well at my checkups." Their thoughts then affect their feelings about the experience.

If you're the person who responds with fear, you'll have physical anxiety reactions including sweaty palms, high blood pressure, and lightheadedness. Your behavior will be different, too. You may skip your appointment or postpone making another one. Your emotional loop will likely repeat itself the next time you get a reminder from the dentist's office.

Here are some more examples of how the emotional loop works. All of them happen in an instant.

Something Threatens You

Suppose you're on your daily walk and a large, angry dog runs toward you, growling and barking. Your *emotion* will be fear. It's instinctual and unconscious. Your physical reactions to anxiety will begin to kick in. You may find yourself shaking and sweating and your pulse increasing. This will happen automatically, too, without you having to think about it.

Next, you have *thoughts* about fear, based on what you already know about this kind of threat. Your brain-computer has stored input about other instances when you've encountered a threat. You may think about another time that an angry dog has run at you or a time when you've seen it happen to someone else.

Then, you have *feelings*. In this case, they will be feelings of panic or dread. These will occur on a conscious level, based on the thoughts you have in reaction to your fear. You anticipate what might happen if the dog gets to you and bites you. In response to these feelings, you turn and run. That's the behavior that your emotions, thoughts, and feelings have prompted.

Something Upsets You

Now, suppose you're at work and someone you've mentored is promoted over you, so they're now your boss. Your *emotion* will be unconscious and instinctual. It will likely be anger. Your blood pressure could rise, and your face may turn red.

Next, you have *thoughts* about your anger. You may recall things that caused you anger at work in the past, like when you got an unfair review or were blamed for a mistake. These thoughts come from your internal database.

Finally, you experience *feelings* of frustration, bitterness, or maybe even fury. You'll be aware of what you're feeling because of the thoughts you've had based on your work history. Your behavior will be based on these feelings, but it can vary. If your feeling is frustration, you may be able to get over it and congratulate your colleague. Or you may hold on to your frustration, go home, and pout. Again, your behavior will be based on your feelings.

Something Good Happens

Say you've received something you've wanted for a long time. Maybe your spouse has surprised you with tickets to Aruba for your anniversary. Immediately, you will experience joy. You won't even think about it yet. You'll simply have automatic, instinctual *emotions* of surprise and happiness. You'll likely smile and gasp automatically and instinctively.

Soon, you'll have *thoughts* about the amazing gift. You'll automatically think about other vacations you've had or maybe your honeymoon in Aruba 10 years ago. These thoughts will be based on experiences you have stored in the recesses of your brain.

In less than a moment, you'll have *feelings*, in this case, excitement and enthusiasm. You express this on a conscious level with your behavior, by expressing a heartfelt thank you and kissing your spouse.

Comparing Emotional Loops

Emotional loops can be different, depending on the maturity level of a person and what they have stored in their internal database. Consider this scenario.

A crocodile is approaching a boatful of people. One of the passengers notices. They will have an automatic emotion of fear. Their thoughts will be based on their knowledge of what crocodiles can do. The feelings this arouses are likely to be panic, dread, and horror.

Now, think about a toddler who is also a passenger on the boat. They may never have had any experience of a crocodile, never even seen one in a picture book. Let's say that the child hasn't noticed the other people's reaction to the creature. The toddler will instantaneously experience fear anyway. Why?

The child has no prior memories or understanding. What they do have is an instinctive fear of the unknown. Because of this, they will unconsciously experience the emotion of fear.

The child will still have automatic thoughts about the situation. They won't be based on any actual experiences with crocodiles since they don't have any. Their database doesn't have anything in it that corresponds to what's happening. Their thoughts will be more along the lines of *There's something I don't know that is coming toward me. Why is it doing that? It's scary looking. What is going to happen? I think I may need protection. Where is someone who can help me?*

The toddler will then feel fright, panic, or anxiety. They will likely begin crying or screaming.

Next, the child will notice the grownups' reactions and file this away in their own database of experiences and memories. The next time they see a crocodile, they will have something that will inform their reaction. Their response will still be instinctual and unconscious, but it will have a basis in reality.

Basically, young children have the same emotions as adults—fear, anger, joy, and so forth. They just don't have the vocabulary to express what they're feeling or the life experiences to have an extensive database of memories and thoughts that can give them perspective.

Children's emotions are often stronger and more purely positive or negative than adults'. As they grow and experience more and more varied stimuli, they build their database and have more sophisticated thoughts and feelings.

What This Means for Human Comprehension

Learning is an essential part of your journey through life. You learn from every bit of stimulus that enters your brain algorithms. Then the brain recalculates what's already been stored in the light of the new information. This renewed comprehension and all the connections that have been made are the essence of your individuality.

Your mind is constantly evolving. In the first chapter, I described the brain's synapses, the way connections are made between the neurons so that they can pass along electrical and chemical signals to one another. Trillions of these synapses are constantly forming and re-forming. If they're not used, they die off. Thus, the brain is continuously evolving.

In the first two chapters, you've discovered that what we know about the brain and our emotions, thoughts, and feelings is changing. The experts don't all agree about what is going on inside the brain, so don't be alarmed if you don't understand it all, either. Like your brain algorithms, knowledge about the brain is being discovered, analyzed, and reorganized, over and over again.

What does this all mean for you? Well, what *is* known about how our emotions, thoughts, and feelings work is that these brain functions are only partly understood. But what we do know emphasizes how complicated and wonderful our brains are, and it reveals a lot about the level of emotional awareness that's needed to produce desired behavior.

This is all important information when you're dealing with challenges that require a certain amount of life-work to understand. Major life issues and trauma can severely affect the way you live and your quality of life. There can be significant grief when you determine the root causes that have propelled you into the state you are in now. You can learn new ways of changing your comprehension.

It happens like this: Your thoughts and feelings profoundly influence one another. You then behave in a certain way. As I mentioned in the previous chapter, you can retrain or reprogram your brain so that you don't get stuck in this emotional loop. With guidance, if you can challenge your thought process and change it, you change how you feel about a certain stimulus in turn. When your feelings change, especially if they become less intense, your behavior can become more positive as a result. This will help you cope with the adversities you encounter in daily life.

Grief Brain

There's a phenomenon known as "grief brain." It happens when grief overwhelms your mental processing, and you go on automatic. The things you do without thinking about them can be irrational. You might find yourself putting the newspaper in the refrigerator, for example, or forgetting where you left your glasses, even if they're on the top of your head. You could find yourself forgetting to pay bills or paying them twice.

Things that used to come easily to you may not for a while. Your concentration, memory, decision-making, and cognitive abilities suffer, and you may experience everything happening in a fog. Your brain is on overload.

The disruptions of neurotransmitters and hormones that grief brain causes can also have negative effects on your sleeping patterns, the quality of your sleep, your appetite, and your energy level. You simply don't interact with your environment in the same way that you do when you're functioning normally. Your brain is focused on the emotions and thoughts of your loss, and it just doesn't have room for your normal tasks. You might even have difficulty expressing yourself, even though that's something you may need to do.

If this happens to you, be gentle with yourself. It's a normal reaction to grief that will eventually pass. When you do make an important decision or react to a stimulus in a rational manner, you should applaud yourself for accomplishing it. And when you don't, cut yourself some slack.

You can use simple techniques like writing a checklist of things you need to do and crossing them off as you do them. Remember that you don't have to do them all in the order you wrote them down. And don't think you have to do everything yourself. If you have a sympathetic friend or family member, let them take part of the load off you.

What's Next?

Now that you have explored the powerful basics of the human brain and the interactions between emotions, thoughts, and feelings, it's time to turn your attention to what causes grief and what your reactions to it might be.

First, we'll tackle one of the most common emotions that accompanies grief: anxiety. Anxiety is rough on both your body and your brain. Your brain affects the body systems that govern anxiety, from the stress hormones that bring it on to the detrimental physical effects. But is anxiety your friend or your foe? In the next chapter, you'll find out.

Depression is another consequence of grief that can be debilitating. You'll learn about all the different kinds of depression and learn to recognize the symptoms. Like anxiety, depression affects both your body and mind.

Then, we'll look at some common causes of grief. If you're experiencing the loss of a relationship through estrangement or divorce, grief is a natural reaction. If you are troubled by financial hardship or poverty, you'll also have accompanying grief.

All these topics will be addressed in Section 2 of this book: Major Life Events.

Section 2:

Major Life Events

Chapter 4: Anxiety—Friend and Foe

The greatest glory in living lies not in never falling, but in rising every time we fall. —
Nelson Mandela

In This Chapter

Grief wears many hats! You can experience grief when major life events occur, even ones that don't involve death. That grief is often complicated by anxiety. This is one of the emotions that all of us share, and it's crucial for well-being and survival. But when you develop severe or panic-level anxiety, it becomes a serious problem.

What Is Anxiety?

The American Psychological Association (2022) defines anxiety as "an emotion characterized by feelings of tension, worried thoughts, and physical changes like increased blood pressure." Most people think of anxiety as a bad thing. It has detrimental effects on the human body, including high blood pressure and migraines. It messes with your mind and emotions as well. Anxiety can interfere with your ability to love someone, to cope with setbacks, and to approach daily life.

Still, anxiety is a natural emotion and has its uses. It keeps you from doing things that can cause you harm. It can alert you to dangers that you need to react to. And it can let you know that you are in emotional trouble.

So, is anxiety your friend or your foe? Really, it can be either one, depending on the circumstances. The problem is differentiating between when it's harmful and when it's helpful. Let's take a look at why that's true.

Anxiety Is Your Friend

Anxiety is an ancient instinct. It's been around since human life began and has continued to affect everyone right up until modern times. In the past, anxiety was a reaction that helped to keep the human species alive. Without it, we might not even be here!

Early humans faced many challenges in their everyday lives. Threats lurked everywhere. People faced those threats, but they had anxiety to help them. How?

Consider the large, dangerous animals that can kill a person with one swipe of their paws or one bite from their sharp teeth. At any moment, one of these threats could appear and potentially take the life of anyone who wasn't paying attention.

So, early humans paid attention. They used their keen senses to tell them when a deadly threat was near. They picked up signals such as faint sounds, sights, and smells that indicated a predator was approaching. They could see or hear the rustling of an animal stalking through the brush. They could smell the distinctive scent given off by a hungry saber-toothed tiger or a marauding gorilla.

Those signals resulted in anxiety. The early humans may not even consciously have sensed the presence of the threat. The subtle clues probably entered their senses subliminally. They would have thought: *Something threatening is in the area*, not *That's a leopard sneaking up on me*. They would have reacted to the danger by moving to the safety of a cave, a fire, or a larger group of their tribe that could help them escape or eliminate the threat. It was anxiety that kept them alive.

Of course, in modern life, saber-toothed tigers aren't much of a problem anymore but there are plenty of other threats that can jeopardize your safety or even your life. Think about driving on a highway, for example. A reckless driver could easily cause a deadly accident. Your senses are attuned to potential threats. You hear an engine revving behind you, see the flash of a speeding car in your peripheral vision, or smell the exhaust from a semi that's braking suddenly in front of you.

You anticipate danger and react with anxiety, which prepares you to take evasive action. You check your rearview mirror, slow down or speed up, or move to the other lane. Once the danger is past, you breathe a sigh of relief and notice that your hands are shaking. These are natural reactions that give hints of the anxiety that may have just saved your life. Your brain processes the information from your senses faster than you can even think about danger, and it reacts to avoid it.

Anxiety also appears in situations that are not life or death. You experience anxiety because you think your boss is going to give you a bad review. You experience anxiety when you realize you don't have time to study for your final exam. You experience anxiety when you leave your child alone with a new babysitter. Those are all situations in which something bad could happen. Your anxiety alerts you to the possibility so that you can take steps to prevent a negative outcome.

Anxiety Is Your Foe

Sometimes, though, your anxiety is exaggerated, out of sync with the degree of the threat that you face. Your mind and body still react with anxiety symptoms (which I'll discuss in a moment). You become jumpy, and other people notice this. That can add to your anxiety, creating a feedback loop that just gets worse and worse. It can affect your ability to cope with the stresses of everyday life.

You can also suffer from irrational behavior caused by your anxiety. For example, in the case of a person who develops anxiety on the highway, an irrational behavior might be refusing to ever drive on the highway. The person afraid of a bad review at work might quit their job and look for a new one before they come up for review. The student running out of time to study might waste more time going to a bar, trying to calm their nerves with alcohol.

When your anxiety is prolonged, the effects can be so serious that you need to see a doctor. A medical doctor or a mental health professional may be required to help you deal with it and the effects it has.

Next, I'll discuss the physical effects of anxiety on the human body.

The Biology of Anxiety

Regardless of whether anxiety is your friend or your foe, it has specific effects on your body. It impacts your brain, circulatory system, digestion, breathing, muscles, and more. The longer the anxiety goes on, the more severe the effects are.

How does anxiety have such striking effects? It's because anxiety triggers the body's fight-or-flight response. In threatening situations, this response is understandable and helpful. But if the anxiety goes on even after the threat has disappeared, it keeps your body in this mode.

Your body responds to threats with changes that can help you face the fear that a dangerous situation causes. Your pulse and breathing increase, which sends oxygenated blood to your brain and muscles, priming them to react. The brain and body release adrenaline and cortisol, which are stress hormones that lead to these bodily changes. This is an appropriate reaction to fear.

When you're not in immediate danger, though, these bodily responses are not appropriate. You don't need to fight or flee, so you don't need your pulse and breathing to speed up. Adrenaline and cortisol are not necessary, but your body keeps pumping them out anyway. When blood is directed away from your body's core—the muscles and organs in the torso—and rushes to your brain and extremities, it stays there, and the physiological changes continue. Your blood pressure and pulse remain high, for example.

The symptoms of anxiety mimic the body's reactions to danger and fear. Your hands shake, you feel nauseous, your muscles tense up, you become pale, you sweat profusely, and you have an increased pulse rate. All these reactions put strain on your body, especially if they continue for a long time. You aren't able to concentrate on anything else other than whatever is causing your anxiety.

If you're reacting to a real, physical danger, these effects wear off when the threat has passed. If your anxiety continues for a long time, however, your body can be damaged. You can develop chest pain and heart trouble if your pulse stays too fast for too long. Muscle tension can cause backaches and headaches. The stress hormones in your brain can lead to insomnia. Fatigue is another natural consequence, as your body has been in overdrive and unable to rest and relax. You can lose interest in sex, develop depression, or have suicidal thoughts. Anxiety can even impair your immune function, making you more vulnerable to colds, flu, and other infections.

You can suffer these ill effects of anxiety if you are involved in an ongoing stressful situation. A divorce, for example, is usually stressful and often drags out for a long time. You find yourself constantly thinking about aspects of it, such as custody of the children and alimony but also the hurt and anger you feel and the uncertainty of where and how you'll live afterward. This stress can continue for months or even years. Just seeing your former spouse can flood your body with stress hormones.

If you have an underlying health condition, such as arteries that are clogged by cholesterol or the consequences of alcoholism or addiction to drugs, the physical effects of stress and anxiety will multiply. The damage these other conditions cause will increase because of anxiety and stress. The longer the anxiety lasts, the more damage will be done. I'll have more to say about this later.

It's worth noting that the negative effects of stress may not appear right away. They may be simmering below the surface for months or years, then unexpectedly pop up later. You may think you have left the stress behind, but it can remain, eating away at you as you carry on with your life. Your doctor might even treat symptoms like cardiovascular problems without understanding that they are caused by the ongoing anxiety you feel.

The Psychology of Anxiety

Anxiety has negative effects on your mental and emotional functioning as well. As you can imagine, long-term anxiety can interfere with your psychological functioning. Day-to-day stresses cause momentary disruptions in your thinking and emotions. These responses don't last very long because the stress usually disappears before long.

Long-term anxiety is something else. Instead of a temporary disruption, severe, ongoing anxiety magnifies your problems. You might become irritable about things that wouldn't have bothered you before the stress kicked in. This can damage your relationships with coworkers or family members, making everyone unhappy, including you. Rather than being momentarily distracted, you could become completely scattered and unable to concentrate. This can have a snowball effect, too. If you can't concentrate, you may start making mistakes at work, which will only increase your anxiety further.

Your feelings really take a beating when you suffer from chronic anxiety. You may experience any number of unpleasant symptoms. You may feel detached from reality. You could start experiencing fear that something bad will happen. You could develop a whole new crop of anxieties such as fear that other people are angry with you. You could become overly needy and clingy. You could give in to overthinking, replaying bad events over and over in your mind. You may even have anxiety about anxiety itself and stress about what it's doing to you.

Anxiety can also affect the way you relate to others. You might withdraw from people and avoid social occasions you would ordinarily enjoy. At the end of the workday, you may isolate yourself from your family members, hiding away in your rec room, study, garage, or another little-used room. You might even start having trouble performing your normal day-to-day functions such as eating, grooming, exercising, or going to school or work.

The other potential problem is that you may develop a serious psychological disorder. Your ability to function may be so severely impaired that you have what's commonly called a nervous breakdown but is really a condition that requires treatment from a mental health professional. If this happens to you, you aren't going crazy! You're simply suffering from the effects of stress and anxiety.

Anxiety Disorders

Anxiety isn't one single psychological disorder. There are many different conditions that involve stress and anxiety. Depending on the cause of your anxiety and the length of time you've lived with it, you could develop any of a variety of disorders. Which one you suffer from depends on your particular circumstances and your general psychological makeup.

Your family history is one factor that can affect your psychological condition. So is your habitual way of dealing with difficulties—whether you tend to avoid them or dive right in and try to fix everything. Each of the following conditions manifests in different ways and requires different kinds of treatment. The common denominator is that they are all ways that cause your mental health to suffer if you don't get your anxiety under control.

Controlling your anxiety is easier said than done, of course. If you could do it by yourself, you wouldn't be experiencing the negative physical and mental effects. You don't have to suffer in silence, though. Help for anxiety disorders is available.

Generalized Anxiety Disorder

The most common type of condition that arises from prolonged stress is generalized anxiety disorder (GAD). When you have GAD, you have anxiety even when there is nothing in particular in your life that should cause you concern. You feel fear, worry, and stress anyway. You could have a mild case or a more severe one that bothers you almost every day. It's diagnosed when a case lasts for six months or longer, with three or more symptoms.

The Anxiety and Depression Association of America [ADAA] (2022) puts the number of people suffering from GAD at about 6.8 million adults every year. However, less than half of those people are under treatment for it. While genetics and biological factors may play a role in GAD, most often it's a result of excessive stress.

Some people who have GAD think it's simply a part of their everyday personality—that it's just the way they are. GAD can develop in childhood or early adulthood, so a person may have experienced it for most of their life. They don't understand the emotional worry cycle (see Chapter 3) and feel that their anxiety is out of control. Because they're not able to control the causes of their worry, people with GAD may try to plan and control their circumstances, even when that's not possible.

Social Anxiety Disorder

Almost everyone has anxiety about public speaking or any activity involving an audience. Fortunately, for most people, these events don't happen very often. With social anxiety disorder (SAD), the affected person's stress focuses on more common social interactions. They fear being embarrassed or humiliated in a social situation such as a party, dinner, or a work-related event.

It's not the same as simple shyness, however. Sufferers anticipate being judged and rejected. It can result in feeling ashamed and alone. Someone with SAD may realize that their anxiety is exaggerated, but they may be unable to control it. Ironically, their anxiety may result in physical symptoms such as their hands shaking. That makes having dinner with friends, for example, even more of a cause for anxiety.

SAD can appear as early as the early teen years; it affects approximately 15 million adults. A third of people who suffer from SAD wait 10 years before getting help for the condition, despite the fact that there are effective treatments (ADAA, 2022).

Phobias

Almost everyone has something they're afraid of, from bees or new places to high bridges or needles. Those fears don't really affect their day-to-day lives, though. Phobias, however, are fears that are severe enough to influence a person's everyday life. Phobias such as fear of driving, flying, becoming ill, or visiting the dentist are more likely to interfere with everyday functioning and can have serious consequences. For example, you might not be able to take a good job that you've been offered if it requires travel. If you fear going to the dentist, your dental health may suffer, leading to tooth loss. A person with a phobia may realize that their fear is irrational, but they're unable to shake it off. Even thinking about the trigger can cause fear.

Phobias can develop as early as childhood but are also likely to appear in young adulthood. They're likely to arise with little to no warning. Women are known to develop phobias more than men do. According to the ADAA (2022) more than 9% of people in the US are affected by phobias.

Obsessive-Compulsive Disorder

Obsessive-compulsive disorder (OCD) is a condition that is widely misunderstood. Some people use the term to refer to those who seem overly tidy or precise. In reality, it can be a serious disorder. Someone with OCD suffers from obsessions such as cleanliness, or from compulsions such as counting or rearranging objects.

The person may realize that their obsession or compulsion makes no real sense, but they feel anxiety if they don't perform their ritual. Others have rituals that seem better connected, such as a person obsessed with germs who has a ritual of excessive hand-washing. A person with OCD feels no satisfaction in performing their obsessive rituals. They do feel a lessening of stress, however.

OCD typically appears during the teen years (though it sometimes appears by age 10), with females being three times more likely than males to suffer from the disorder. Symptoms can appear gradually or suddenly. It's not a very common disorder; less than 3% of the U.S. population has it (ADAA, 2022). As such, it is difficult to diagnose, and other anxiety disorders are often mistaken for OCD. Without treatment, the condition can last for decades, impairing a person's ability to function in everyday life.

Panic Disorder

Panic attacks appear spontaneously at any time—even when we first wake up in the morning. Panic disorder can happen when a person experiences fear, fright, or terror that's not associated with any triggering event. It's considered a disorder when someone experiences panic symptoms frequently and worries about having another panic attack to the extent that it interferes with their everyday functioning.

Panic disorder can be very distressing. For example, it can cause a person to miss work, go to the doctor frequently, or avoid places where they fear they might have an attack. Symptoms of attacks include having a rapid pulse and chest pain, sweating, and experiencing difficulty breathing. It can also cause insomnia and general irritability. For a diagnosis of panic disorder, conditions such as thyroid problems and other medical conditions need to be ruled out.

The ADAA (2022) notes that as many as 3% of people may have panic disorder, with women twice as likely to have it as men. There are treatments that can help with the condition once it is correctly diagnosed.

Acute Stress Disorder and Post-Traumatic Stress Disorder

Acute stress disorder happens in the aftermath of a traumatic event such as a car crash, and it lasts for several weeks to a month. If symptoms, including anxiety and depression, continue for longer than that, it's considered to be PTSD. This condition doesn't have to occur immediately after the trauma. Often, it appears much later. It can also be intermittent, coming and going unpredictably.

Events that can result in PTSD are seriously distressing experiences such as natural disasters, war, or rape. Symptoms include intrusive memories of the traumatic event, distressing dreams, dissociative reactions such as flashbacks, physical or mental reactions to reminders of the incidents, blame of self or others, trouble with family or other relationships, feelings of anger or shame, and lack of interest in pleasurable activities.

Although most people think of PTSD in the context of war veterans, women are twice as likely to experience it as men. First responders and police officers are also subject to PTSD. Around 12 million U.S. adults suffer from PTSD in any given year, with more than 6% having it at some point during their lives (ADAA, 2022). PTSD has received a lot of attention lately because the effects are so severe, enough to be completely disabling.

Social Isolation

During and after the COVID-19 pandemic, people became more aware of the problems of loneliness and social isolation. Of course, these conditions didn't start with the pandemic. They've been around for years. Anyone can experience loneliness, from schoolchildren to senior citizens. Social isolation is a larger problem that can be experienced by anyone, but it is particularly significant among the elderly population, as well as people who live or work in remote locations.

In general, loneliness is a measure of the quality of a person's social network, while social isolation depends on the number of social connections that someone has. Conditions that often accompany social isolation are depression and low self-esteem. Consequences include increased rates of dementia, stroke, heart disease, and stress and sleep disorders.

Exact statistics on how many people suffer from social isolation are hard to come by, but the ADAA's (2022) estimates put the number at 20% of the general population and more than 40% of seniors. Doctors can and should screen for loneliness and social isolation when they see older patients.

Related Illnesses and Disabilities

Anxiety disorders are also possible in people who have physical illnesses and physical or mental disabilities. The challenges of dealing with everyday life mean that many people experience frustration, depression, and anxiety. Chronic, long-term conditions make the presence of anxiety disorders more likely. I'll discuss these circumstances more in an upcoming chapter.

The ADAA's statistics are hardly definitive because of the number of people who suffer in silence, not seeking treatment. The actual numbers could be higher, meaning that the problem of anxiety disorders is even more widespread.

Seeking Help

The outlook for people with anxiety disorders is generally very good if they seek treatment. I've counseled many people with these disorders, especially those who've had social phobias, acute stress disorders, or PTSD. Their geographic and social isolation left them emotionally numb and detached from their own feelings. Despite their loneliness, they had become anxious or panicky when they thought about social interaction.

In my experience, a high percentage of people don't seek help for anxiety disorders right away. Most of the cases I've worked on were brought to my attention by concerned friends, loved ones, or neighbors. Professional ethics meant I never imposed my counseling services on them—all my clients had to agree to see me. The only exceptions were several occasions when a doctor requested an appointment for their patient because of the risk of self-harm.

People with anxiety disorders shun the limelight and go to great pains to avoid interaction. Also, they will desperately try to downplay or hide their disorder or phobia. It takes a great deal of time to develop their trust and confidence. Sometimes, it might take several appointments before a client feels comfortable enough with the client-counselor relationship that they feel they can divulge very much about what is happening in their life.

People with anxiety problems are at an increased risk of developing depression, which I'll discuss in the next chapter. If anxiety problems are not addressed, the symptoms are likely to continue and worsen, with significant life-diminishing consequences.

I advise people who are experiencing symptoms consistent with an anxiety disorder to seek professional help. Not only is there a high risk of developing depression, but the techniques used to reduce symptoms need to be monitored by an experienced mental health professional. I'll discuss these techniques and strategies in a later chapter.

You should remember that this book is a guide to what happens in professional treatment, not a do-it-yourself instruction manual. Some of the techniques would be stressful to attempt without an experienced professional to guide you through them. Also, if you're suffering from an anxiety disorder, you may be unaware of the condition and its underlying causes. It can also be very upsetting to work through the life issues that cause anxiety behaviors. An experienced professional will develop a structured plan specifically for you and make changes based on any progress or setbacks you experience.

Samantha's Story

I was contacted one day by a woman who had been concerned about her friend Samantha for some time. She was quite distressed and had even contacted the police at one stage to check on her friend's welfare. She told me that this had only made Samantha detach even more.

I called Samantha to check on her welfare, and she agreed to see me. After a couple of appointments, we were developing a good client-professional relationship, and we were able to work on some interpersonal and cognitive behavior therapy (CBT), which included a desensitization program. We identified the root cause of Samantha's anxiety disorder, which stemmed from the end of her marriage eight years previously.

She had associated grief from the divorce which she had suppressed, as well as developed subsequent behavior. There were no children. Samantha's husband and his friends had been her entire social network. In fact, the woman who referred Samantha to me was one of Samantha's former husband's friends. After the divorce, she stopped associating with everyone, first friends and then society in general.

Samantha's anxiety became chronic, progressing to the point where she would hide from anyone who walked up her driveway. She would drive almost 40 miles to a neighboring town several times a month for groceries rather than shopping locally. Her anxiety and isolation were simply devastating.

Our appointments continued once a week for five months. There was slow progress at first. But it was amazing how eager for social connections Samantha became once she gained a certain level of confidence. Our desensitization exercises continued and progressed.

One of her homework exercises was to have coffee at her place with the woman who had initially contacted me.

Eventually, Samantha's transformation was profound. The coffee date alone was an amazing shift toward recovery. After therapy, Samantha was able to return to a life without too much anxiety—essentially, a changed life.

A year or so after our appointments, Samantha contacted me to thank me. She called to tell me that the bitterness between her and her ex-husband had stopped. Now, they were able to have civil conversations whenever they crossed paths. This was real progress.

Samantha had become able to make social connections—even with her ex-husband—all thanks to starting a carefully constructed therapy process. Now, Samantha is proving that the strategies she learned have become life lessons. She now has increased emotional awareness. Once that is mastered and becomes second nature, real emotional growth happens, and anxiety and grief lose their grip on a person like Samantha.

Chapter 5:
Depression—Pandemic Proportions

We all have mental health in the same way that we all have physical health. It's okay to have depression, it's okay to have anxiety, it's okay to have an adjustment disorder. –Prince Harry

In This Chapter

Depression is one of the most common mental health problems in the world today. The serious overuse of the word "depression" has led many people to disregard the symptoms—as if they are normal for most people. Depression is not just feeling sad or a bit gloomy and down from time to time. It's a very serious illness.

Depression Is a Universal Problem

What most people call depression is part of the natural human condition. Everyone feels depressed sometimes. But when depression continues for too long, as it might after a traumatic circumstance or event, it becomes a psychological problem that requires professional help. In serious or clinical depression, a person is not able to escape the effects on their own. And the effects are devastating and life changing.

As with many serious psychological conditions, depression becomes a real problem when it interferes with a person's day-to-day functioning. People with depression may not be able to take care of themselves. They may isolate themselves from other people, which will only make the condition worse. They may begin crying at any time, even if there's no obvious reason to. That's when it's time to seek help. And you can't just snap out of depression by yourself. You will need a professional to make progress.

What Is Depression?

Clinical depression, also called major depression or major depressive disorder (MDD), is different from the everyday experience of being sad. It's a mood disorder, a medical and psychological condition that involves persistent, long-lasting sadness and a lack of interest in activities you previously enjoyed. But it's much more than that.

Depression is an illness of the brain. There are significant changes in the brain of a depressed person that can produce changes in both their thinking and their bodily functions. This is a very serious mental illness. Not addressing it will only make it last longer and make the condition worse. In extreme cases, it can lead to death: It's a major cause of suicide.

If you have experienced a traumatic event, whether that be the death of a loved one, a divorce, estrangement from a family member, the death of a child, the loss of your home caused by a natural disaster, loss of a job, or another major life disruption, you are at risk of major depression.

The statistics are telling. Worldwide, 280 million people have suffered from depression in the past year; in the US, at least 17.3 million adults over the age of 18 are victims of the disorder, but it can affect young children and teens as well. It's the leading cause of disability for those aged 15 and up. It affects twice as many women as men. And when it comes to getting treatment for depression, nearly 40% of adults simply don't (ADAA, n.d.).

The symptoms of depression differ. In general, people with depression feel sad, lonely, and scared. They feel empty, hopeless, or pessimistic. They may feel fatigued yet have trouble sleeping. Most serious of all are thoughts of death or suicide attempts. Both men and women can experience these symptoms, but other ones are more specific by gender and age. Men can become angry, irritable, tired, or abuse drugs or alcohol. Women can experience guilt and feelings of worthlessness. Young children may avoid school, experience separation anxiety, or fear that their parents will die. Teens can be surly and have academic trouble. Older adults may have medical problems as well as grief or sadness.

Depression can affect anyone; no one is immune. Life events, changes in the brain, and heredity are common factors. Although depression can run in families, it doesn't mean that if a family member has had it, you automatically will, too. Your life circumstances and brain chemistry are stronger contributing factors.

Personal factors are also likely to have an influence on whether you will develop depression. Your normal personality is one. If you are naturally negative and self-critical, have low self-esteem, worry constantly, or are especially troubled when someone criticizes you, you're more likely to respond to life events by developing major depression.

Depression, the Brain, and the Body

Depression can even make physical changes in the human brain. Recently, MRI studies have documented some of them. Gray matter changes have been seen in the frontal lobe, parietal lobe, thalamus, temporal lobes, hippocampus, and amygdala. White matter also shows signs of shrinking. All these are vital parts of the brain that affect thought and emotions and have numerous connections with each other. Problems with these connections play a part in MDD. Brain inflammation is another likely component. There are effects such as irrational thinking and other cognitive impairments. Researchers hope that future studies will help in finding treatments for depression. More studies of the causes and effects are needed, of course (Pilmeyer et al., 2022).

Neurotransmitters in the brain such as dopamine, serotonin, and norepinephrine also help regulate mood. In depression, the balance between them changes. When depression is relieved, the neurotransmitters may return to their normal state. Other changes in the brain can also return to normal after the depression pulls back.

Inflammation and reduced oxygen in the body are also associated with depression. Disruption of the sleep-wake cycle (circadian rhythm) is implicated, too. Chest pains, chronic joint pain, gastrointestinal symptoms, and appetite changes are all bodily signs that depression may be present. In fact, getting treatment for the physical symptoms is often what brings a patient in for depression treatment. Primary care physicians often give their patients a depression screening inventory when they come in with physical ailments. Then, physicians can identify their depression and patients can get treatment.

Types of Depression

There is more than one kind of major depression besides MDD. Each of them shares things in common with the others, such as major symptoms and effects on a person's life including the ability to care for themselves or hold a job, but there are differences. They affect different groups of people under different circumstances. Here's a look at the most troubling.

Major Depressive Disorder

MDD is the most common and perhaps the most devastating version of the disease. The World Health Organization says that "mental disorders account for 13% of the global disease burden, and major depression alone is expected to be the largest contributor by 2030" (Hock et al., 2012). That's if it isn't already!

The aftereffects of the COVID-19 pandemic include major depression. The worry and enforced isolation, plus the effects of the disease itself, have caused the number of people with depression to rise dramatically. Because of the anxiety that the pandemic has caused, it's been easy to overlook major depression as a consequence.

But MDD isn't something that just came into being with the pandemic. It's been around for many, many years. Why it appears isn't completely known, and several theories vary in popularity. MDD may be caused by genetics; an imbalance in neurotransmitters; physical, sexual, or emotional abuse; or even inflammation. A combination of these factors is also a possibility.

Persistent Depressive Disorder

Depression that lasts for two years or longer is called persistent depressive disorder. The term can manifest as two conditions: dysthymia (low-grade persistent depression) or chronic major depression. The symptoms are similar to the usual symptoms of depression but can often include very low self-esteem and feelings of hopelessness. Although the symptoms are like those of MDD, they're usually less severe but longer lasting. There can also be significant cognitive impairment affecting concentration and decision-making. It's a chronic condition that can last for years. It can strike during childhood, making a child irritable or annoyed as well as depressed.

You may think that symptoms of persistent depressive disorder are just part of your personality—that you're someone who simply has a gloomy outlook on life. Or you may think that the symptoms will always be with you. But they don't have to be. A medical doctor, a psychological practitioner, or even a teacher, faith leader, or trusted friend can set you on the road to mental wellness.

Bipolar Disorder

Bipolar disorder, which used to be called manic depression, has two components. One is mania or hypomania, which involves powerful feelings of euphoria and extremely high energy, but the other part is dysthymia (less severe depression) or major depression. This mood disorder involves swings between the two. It can be severely debilitating. Bipolar disorder is often misdiagnosed as depression, anxiety, or both. Psychosis, including delusions or hallucinations, can also appear.

Many people assume that the manic phase is enjoyable or an occasion to get things done rather than a problem. But mania can lead to destructive, irresponsible behavior such as gambling, overspending, reckless sex, or drug use. The consequences can be severe—financial ruin, broken relationships, or even homelessness.

Seasonal Affective Disorder

This is not the same as when people say they have "the winter blues." Seasonal affective disorder (SAD) is a form of depression that most often occurs during the winter months and typically goes away in spring and summer. At times, people do get fed up with winter weather, but when they have SAD, it's a real reaction to this seasonal period that makes them mentally unwell. It's also possible, however, that a person has symptoms during a different season of the year such as spring. Some people use light therapy—full-spectrum lighting—as a way to alleviate seasonal depression. Simply waiting for the feeling to pass may be tempting, but it opens you up to unnecessary suffering.

Psychotic Depression

Depression can be accompanied by psychosis. Symptoms include hallucinations, delusions, and sometimes severe paranoia. Delusions are a belief in things that aren't likely to be true and having hallucinations means seeing or hearing things that aren't there. Someone suffering from psychotic depression may also appear restless or fidgety. They're definitely at risk for suicide. Like schizophrenia, which it resembles, it's very serious and can incapacitate someone who suffers from it. Medication with antipsychotics and antidepressants, counseling or CBT, social support, or brief hospitalization may be necessary.

Peripartum or Postpartum Depression

Also known as postnatal depression, postpartum depression is major depression that usually appears in the weeks and months after childbirth or sometimes around the time of the birth itself. Many women experience the "baby blues" for a few days to a couple of weeks after giving birth, but postpartum depression is longer lasting and more severe. It interferes with the ability to bond with the baby. Approximately 10% of women experience the more extreme version of depression (Fields, 2021). Women who develop postpartum depression have been known to have hallucinations and delusions and to think about harming their children—or actually harming them.

It's important to get help if you don't feel better after two weeks instead of waiting for your six-week checkup. Counseling, antidepressants, or a synthetic hormone may help you get past the symptoms.

Premenstrual Dysphoric Disorder

People may make jokes about women whose personalities change during their period, but depression at the start of periods is a real thing. "Dysphoric" is a term meaning "depressive." It's the opposite of "euphoric." Women may experience moodiness, irritability, insomnia, and crying spells that appear within the week preceding a menstrual period. The symptoms usually back off once the period starts, and they're more severe than those associated with PMS. Antidepressant medication is one possible treatment. As always, talk to your doctor before you stop taking a medication.

Situational Depression

Depression can also be caused by distressing events that happen in your life, such as experiencing the death of a loved one (or even a pet), getting a divorce, losing a job or starting a new one, getting into a car accident, going into retirement, being present at or the victim of a crime, living through a natural disaster, suffering the effects of the recent pandemic, or receiving the diagnosis of a serious illness. The depression may not show up immediately after the traumatic event, but it can develop later, even a few months afterward. The changes that happen in your life after a distressing event can trigger situational depression. It can improve with the passage of time.

Although situational depression can go away on its own, techniques such as exercise, meditation, relaxation, deep breathing, journaling, paying attention to your diet, and practicing mindfulness can help it ease more quickly. I'll discuss these techniques in Section 3 of this book. Of course, if the depression lasts for a long time, seeing a physician or mental health specialist may be necessary.

Atypical Depression

People with atypical depression have a certain set of symptoms: having insomnia or, paradoxically, sleeping too much; seeing a change in weight (either up or down); feeling restless or rundown; having trouble concentrating or making decisions; and being especially sensitive to rejection. With atypical depression, you can feel a temporary lightening of your mood when there's a pleasurable event like a party. Despite the name "atypical," this condition is actually fairly common. It often begins during the early teen years.

The cause of atypical depression isn't known, but a family history of depression may be one factor. Physical, sexual, or emotional abuse can play a part and so can alcohol or drug abuse. It's twice as likely to affect women as men.

Treatment-Resistant Depression

As the name says, depression can fail to respond to the most common treatments for the condition, such as talk therapy and medication. Your depression may lessen after treatment but then come roaring back. CBT and dialectical behavioral therapy may help, along with changes in medication or medications not ordinarily used with depression, like antipsychotics or thyroid hormones. Specialists have tried other techniques, including transcranial magnetic stimulation, electroconvulsive therapy, vagus nerve stimulation, and ketamine treatment, with varying degrees of success.

Getting Help

Depression often occurs at the same time as anxiety issues or disorders, which makes them both more difficult to treat. The longer a period of anxiety lasts, the more likely it is that the anxiety will change into depression. On the other hand, people with depression have been known to develop anxiety regarding how their lives have changed because of not being diagnosed.

You absolutely *must* seek treatment if you have a depressive disorder. The consequences if you don't are too severe—including suicidal thoughts or attempted or completed suicide. Even if you suspect you may have depression because you show many of the symptoms, getting treatment is essential. The sooner depression is caught, the sooner you can begin recovering from it.

Of course, if you experience symptoms such as cognitive impairment or significant negative changes in your thinking or mood, it can be confusing, and you may not realize that you need help or what to do about your condition. A mental health professional can guide you through the difficulties of treatment.

You can ask your primary care physician or family doctor to recommend a counselor if you are experiencing symptoms. You can also search for practitioners in your area. It's true that many professionals have long waiting lists until they are available. You may be able to get some relief from an online counseling service while you await an appointment.

One of the most effective means of treatment is a combination of talk therapy and medication. There are many antidepressant medications available now. It may take a little time to find what works for you. If medication does not produce the desired result, you should go back and see your doctor again. Sometimes, the process of settling on a medical treatment can take a little bit of tweaking. You may also find there are side effects that trouble you, so a change in the type of medication or an increase or decrease of the dosage may be necessary.

It's also very important to note that medication may not be the answer for every individual. That's for you and your doctor to determine. Also, medication will only allow you to not be so consumed by your emotions. Some people feel that medication dulls their emotions. Because of the potential side effects, it's crucial to continue to report back to your doctor in order to get this part of your treatment right.

Medication is one possible intervention, but the causes and effects of depression will still be present. Medication may allow you time to process what's happening to you without becoming overwhelmed by your emotions.

While depression is a very serious matter, there are real solutions that will give you hope for recovery. Just get to a doctor as soon as you exhibit symptoms to discuss a way forward for you. There is a very good chance of recovery. I'll cover good advice on the subject in Section 3 of this book.

But remember, the first step in recovery is admitting you have a problem. Depression won't go away if you wait. Suffering in silence means that your depression has nothing to prevent it from worsening. It will only deepen and become more difficult to treat. Catching it early and taking steps to alleviate it will help ensure that it won't take over your life.

My Depression Story

I've been subject to depression as well. And I've had to come up with solutions before the disorder completely took over my life.

When my second marriage ended and there was no chance of reconciliation, I experienced a great deal of shock. I believed I was flawed. I had nowhere to live and moved back in with my parents for a couple of months. My parents were very supportive, but they were also very worried because of my emotional state.

I sought medical assistance from my doctor and was prescribed an antidepressant.

After a couple of months, I moved out of my parents' home and found an alternative living situation. I slowly worked through the contributing factors that led to the breakdown of my marriage. It was extremely difficult to come to terms with the loss of the dreams and aspirations I'd had for this marriage, such as the plans for children. Everything was gone. It took me time to work on challenging my thought processes.

To combat my depression, I used to write. I found written expression and writing down my thoughts and feelings, then challenging them and rewriting new and improved thoughts, was great therapy. This is a common technique used in counseling, particularly CBT. I'll cover this and other techniques in the chapters of Section 3.

Writing was very effective for me; the process just took time and a commitment to changing my mindset. I wrote poetry and enjoyed this type of self-expression. I found that it really helped with processing my grief and loss. In time, I also wrote daily affirmations as I started to gain knowledge and control of my emotions. It still took many months before I was able to feel hopeful and confident about life beyond my marriage.

If someone who is suffering from depression either ignores the symptoms or doesn't take steps to address and challenge how they think and feel, the situation can become dire both physically and mentally. Depression can definitely be alleviated, however. Later, in Section 3, you will learn how you can overcome depression. Believe me: The skills and knowledge you acquire will stay with you for life and will help you again and again when life hardships happen.

Chapter 6:
Divorce and Estrangement

You don't have to control your thoughts. You just have to stop letting them control you. –Dan Millman

In This Chapter

When lifelong dreams are shattered by divorce, separation, or estrangement, there is also associated grief. Many of the factors associated with such life issues are intensely stressful and create emotional upheaval.

The Anguish of Divorce

For many people, being married, and perhaps raising children, has been one of their fondest dreams. They may have been envisioning a wedding, marriage, and parenthood since childhood. In fact, in today's society, being in a marriage or another committed relationship is considered the expected life path. Young adults find that they are expected to pair off, and they receive a lot of intrusive questions and hints if they haven't done so by the time they reach a certain age.

You may have lived that dream at some point in your life. You may have enjoyed the excitement of partnership and explored the possibility of having children. You may have looked forward to the life you would build together and all the dreams you had for the future.

But, of course, not every marriage lasts. The unthinkable becomes real, and the marriage or partnership is over. To many people, this comes as a shock. Others may have felt the marriage crumbling for some time. Either way, the realization that a divorce is imminent is a cause for deep distress. Your assumptions about how the rest of your life will go are in ruins. You wonder what has happened.

The four pillars of any relationship are communication, honesty, trust, and respect. When one or more of these elements is missing, it's a sign that the relationship is headed for trouble.

All couples have difficulties, but if they can't communicate about them, the likelihood of solving them decreases, and unpleasant feelings can fester and grow. Without honesty in that communication, there is no way to work out differences. It's as if the two people are playing by different sets of rules, even if they think there is only one. Trust is involved because, no matter how tight a couple is, they will naturally have to be apart at times. Knowing that you can trust your partner to do what they say is vital in so many areas—finances, child-rearing, and marital fidelity, to name just a few. And respect is at the base of all these other qualities. If you don't respect your partner, you're not going to have open communication, honesty in dealing with each other, or trust that you can believe what they say.

When a relationship breaks down, it's usually due to a lack of one or more of these fundamental qualities. To get at what actually caused the breakup, you need to look carefully at how the two people measured up to these ideals. There needs to be a clear perception and perspective on what occurred. Unfortunately, an objective point of view is often missing. The couple will each see things in their own way.

That's when a divorce becomes truly overwhelming and potentially nasty. If two people can't agree on where and why their marriage failed, they're also not likely to get past those differences to part amicably.

Members of a couple will very likely need support to get through this devastating mess. Lawyers can handle the legal implications, but other kinds of support are needed as well. Each person needs to have a support system of some type. This may be friends or relatives that they can turn to for sympathy and understanding, a faith leader who has seen these situations happen before, or even a mental health professional who can assist in dealing with the many issues appropriately. When the goal is working toward emotional recovery, you simply can't expect to go it alone.

In the third section of this book, I'll explain strategies and techniques that will help in the process of moving past the trauma that a divorce has caused.

When You're Estranged

Most married couples have big dreams of having a happy family with at least one or more children. Even before there is a child, spouses make plans and have dreams about what their family will look like and what they'll do together. This fantasy plays a big part in their lives.

If there are children, they're yet another factor that must be considered during a breakup or divorce. Disagreements over how to raise them may have been among the causes of the divorce. The child or children have a relationship with both parents. They are likely to be devastated by the sudden change in family life. Their reactions in the case of a divorce or estrangement will simply accentuate the grief of everyone involved. Children will also need help in getting through the turmoil of divorce—even professional help, especially if the divorce is a particularly difficult one.

Children do add another layer of complexity to the situation. In fact, it's not just a new level of complexity. It's an additional layer of grief. Custody battles are among the messiest parts of a divorce, and it's very difficult to work out a solution that suits everyone. The children are likely to feel as confused and distraught as their parents. It's all too likely that one parent or the other will feel estranged from the kids they've brought into the world. Even if the couple doesn't divorce but decides to live separately, they still have to work out childcare arrangements.

When a divorce involves children, you lose the familiarity, the sense of family, that once existed. The beautiful life plans you'd made have been shattered. All parties will feel very dark emotionally. It will require a tremendous energy investment to arrive at an understanding of what needs to be done first, then next, and next, and so on.

Feeling Grief and Other Emotions

A divorce or estrangement can unleash a flood of emotions. The couple is likely to feel shocked, even if they had both realized that the marriage was in trouble. However, there could also be relief or gratitude that the relationship that caused them so much pain and heartache will soon be over, whether that's by divorce, separation, or estrangement. Even in these cases, though, there is still a lot of grief to work through.

One person may feel grief that something they valued so highly has fallen through. Or they may grieve the loss of the family ties. Grief also enters the picture when a person must admit their own failure at keeping the relationship together. There will be grief in remembering the good times that will never be recreated. And there can be grief that a person has wasted so much of their life on something that was not meant to be.

As with other kinds of grief, there is a process that you must go through, which can include anger, bargaining, denial, disbelief, guilt, sadness, and shock. Not everyone experiences all these emotions, and not everyone experiences them in the same order, but they're the most common ones.

There are other complex emotions to be addressed: resentment (a multilayered combination of hate and disgust), and jealousy (a multilayered combination of envy, insecurity, resentment, and suspicion), for example.

In my counseling practice, I have found that a client will make better progress if they can understand that the many emotions they feel, such as bitterness, anger, resentment, or hate, all come from a base of grief. This gives the client greater clarity and makes it easier for them to focus on developing their emotional awareness and, eventually, to recover.

Then there's experiencing a need for revenge, which, unfortunately, is present in many cases of divorce or estrangement. Revenge itself is not an emotion. Instead, it is a psychological state that can be a disturbing aspect of life-changing events. Dealing with a revenge reaction is a very complicated and often lengthy process that requires the presence of someone with counseling experience. It's not something that a close friend or family member can help you with.

What to Do

I've been stressing the need for professional help in dealing with the cascade of feelings and emotions that come along with divorce or estrangement. Without that help, you will likely have a very difficult time gaining a clear perception and perspective. You could have so much jumbled emotion and even irrational thinking that it can be difficult to address all the dynamics appropriately. Prioritization is also important. Without help, it's difficult to determine what can be addressed immediately and what matters need to be worked out later.

There are many situations that can make it difficult to split up the household: financial difficulties that prevent one person from living on their own, for example. If that's the case, and you and your partner still have to live together, both of you will likely need psychological help to deal with the underlying and ongoing problems.

When you're involved in a divorce or estrangement, you'll definitely need a support system. This can include close friends and family members. But it's important to recognize that someone close to you may have biased opinions on who is at fault in the divorce. They may simply run down the other party. Or they may have other motives, such as the desire to see you "cured" and back to your normal self, even if that means you repressing your feelings to do so.

It should go without saying that if you're the victim of an abusive, dangerous situation, you need to leave as soon as you possibly can. The threat doesn't have to be physical, either. There are other kinds of abuse. Verbal abuse and emotional abuse can be as big a problem and have devastating consequences.

Children are incredibly susceptible to verbal and emotional abuse, which can affect them for the rest of their lives. "Keeping the family together" in these circumstances can do more harm than good. If a couple stays together to help the children deal with their understandable grief, that's one thing, but staying together in an abusive situation is much worse for the kids.

To get out and get help is the best advice I can give. Staying in the situation can leave you open to all kinds of behavior that will only cause further problems. You or your partner can suffer from irrational thinking, heightened emotions, or bargaining behavior that makes it difficult to get through the separation with the least possible interpersonal trauma.

Once you are in a physically safe setting, you will still need psychological help to recover from the abuse—children especially so. You may think that just because you are away from the abuser, you'll be fine. But any kind of abuse leaves its traces on the self. Emotional scars can be as damaging as physical ones. They can prevent you from successfully moving into a new relationship, for example. Even if you live alone afterward, the damage done by abuse will hinder your ability to live a satisfied, happy life. The scars left by abuse will continue to affect you until you finally do get some help from a mental health professional.

The life lessons in Section 3 of this book won't bring about the solution to your problems that you may desire. My intention in presenting them is to help you strengthen your emotional awareness, which will lead to emotional growth. "Fixing" yourself is something that you *can* control.

Anne and John's Story

Anne called me one day to discuss relationship issues between her and her husband. They were a couple in their late 40s who had farmed all their married life. They had adult children who were out on their own, leaving Anne and John with an empty nest. What was particularly concerning was the disdain that appeared when they spoke about each other when the other was absent from the room.

We began separate one-on-one sessions in which they could discuss, in private, what was occurring in their lives. By giving each of them a sense of autonomy, they would be free to express whatever they wished. We would have a couple of these separate sessions, then we would reconvene together to see if we could determine a path forward. During the first week, we conducted two one-on-one sessions. Anne and John were both advised not to discuss their respective appointments afterward.

Briefly, what came from the first individual appointment was that Anne said they had been having marriage problems for many years. She said that she had fallen out of love with her husband. She hated the farm, hated her life, and didn't see any of her friends anymore.

John's private session centered on the farm. It had been decimated by drought. He recognized that his marriage was not going too well and said it was the drought that had caused this. He was on antidepressant medication that Anne knew nothing about.

After the second appointment, they both agreed there was a somewhat different mood in the other. This slight change was due to the release of some negative emotions that each had disclosed to me.

When we decided to continue with both of them together in the same session, there were rules: Only if they wished to, each could have five minutes to express their thoughts and feelings to the other without any interruptions. Then the other one would have the same opportunity. We could go back and forth as long as they wanted, but each had to remain silent and respect the other person's time to speak.

Before too long, and with some prompting from me, they had expressed everything to each other that they had expressed to me in their earlier, separate appointments. It was very emotional for them both, and it was difficult. They both spoke of a great deal of sadness, as well as shock regarding how each was feeling. Anne was also experiencing anger, frustration, and resentment. John was shocked by Anne's view that the marriage was beyond repair. A great deal of negative energy was uncovered.

As our appointments progressed, John shared that he had depression and was secretly trying to cope with it. The only person who knew about this was the doctor who had prescribed antidepressant medication. John felt he was failing as a husband and a provider for the family. He had also developed a mild case of social anxiety, avoiding other farmers in the district whenever possible. Anne had developed social anxiety disorder and displayed signs of depression. She had distanced herself from friends and hated doing the shopping. She had even experienced several panic attacks during or simply when thinking about having to go shopping.

The emotional health of both Anne and John had deteriorated over the previous two years. They hadn't talked about each other's welfare during this time. In fact, they both agreed that there had really been no communication at all.

After the first couple of weeks, we scheduled weekly appointments over several months. When we delved into the root issues that led to the negative behavior they displayed, they certainly expressed grief. I gave the couple an environment in which they could talk about this and have it acknowledged.

This is a crucial step toward healing. There needs to be emotional awareness, and in their own time, Anne and John were able to challenge their thought processes. In couples counseling, giving respect to each other's point of view is also crucial for healing. In time, their grief subsided, and they learned life skills and emotional awareness. Yes, there was still sadness and regret. But they were no longer consumed and controlled by their emotions.

Within 12 months, both Anne and John had worked through and recovered from depression and anxiety and the associated negative behaviors. They both agreed their marriage was still a work in progress, but they both had control over their disorders and were socializing again.

Looking back, Anne and John were suffering from the effects of a lack of communication, honesty, trust, and respect—the four pillars of a relationship. The grief associated with addressing the causes and working back toward emotional recovery took considerable time and effort. In the end, it was worth it.

Andrew's Story

Andrew was referred to me by a child psychologist who had been working with Andrew's estranged children. In my initial appointments with him, he expressed anger and bitterness toward his wife, but even more so toward his mother-in-law regarding the situation he was in. This seemed to be very rational thinking to Andrew from his frame of reference at the time.

It takes energy and commitment to challenge your own thought processes. It only happens when you have some understanding that what you are experiencing is actually irrational thinking. That understanding can take time, and it did for Andrew.

The real turning point came when he had two realizations. First, he was not responsible for or able to control another person's behavior. Up to this point, he had expressed a great deal of negative energy. Then, he understood that this was simply out of his control. A second realization became apparent to Andrew: He didn't want to be controlled by these negative emotions anymore.

He now understood that the behavior of his wife and mother-in-law (justly or unjustly) was controlling his life. The only way for him to achieve peace was to challenge his thought processes. This was not easy. Andrew's determination was driven by the two realizations he had made. I wrote them down in black marking pen and he referred to them, even read them out loud when he needed to.

Andrew required courage when he started to realize that his thoughts about the situation with his wife and mother-in-law were irrational. Once this process had occurred, Andrew had a new understanding that he had to take ownership of what had happened.

The process of changing your thoughts is not a smooth or systematic one. It takes time, perseverance, guidance, and reassurance from an experienced mental health professional. The affected person can at times revert to irrational thinking. It would have been easier for Andrew to project anger and hate onto someone else so that he wouldn't have to take ownership of the incredibly painful situation he was in. Whenever this projection happened, I brought out the piece of paper with the two sentences: You are not responsible for, or able to control, another's behavior. You are being controlled by negative emotions, and those thoughts are controlling your life.

Very quickly, Andrew would revert to recovery mode; he did not wish to be either controlled or out of control anymore. Going back to irrational thoughts is less frequent when the responsibility for what has occurred is owned; there is a level of acceptance.

Remember that we are retraining the brain, programming this sophisticated human-computer. It takes time to challenge and then change your thought process when your thinking is irrational. There is no magic bullet that gives you the desired outcomes. The secret is to focus on yourself. The rest is out of your control.

This was the next step of acceptance for Andrew. He was progressing well with his emotional awareness. Self-actualization gathers momentum when desired, positive behavior is the result of rational thoughts and feelings. Yes, Andrew still suffered disillusionment as he touched base with me every few months. He also still hadn't reunited with his children.

However, with his new comprehension, Andrew soon was able to have empathy for his children. He was able to put himself in their shoes and understand their point of view. He started to realize that their frame of reference was out of his control. It was a huge mind shift. There was sadness, yes, but also acceptance.

Andrew remained vigilant regarding his self-improvement and self-actualization. He used the techniques and life skills that he had learned, and he developed rituals like journaling his thoughts and behaviors. He had become his own best friend. (I'll have more to say about this in Section 3.)

In time, Andrew reconnected with his children and started a new relationship with a woman he had met. The last time we spoke, Andrew shared something with me. He said that he had told his new girlfriend all that had happened in his life that had led to his marriage breakdown and estrangement from his children.

His exact words were, "I took a risk. I knew I could lose her. I told her everything and owned my own shit." Andrew went on to say, "I didn't want anything to bite me in the ass, so I put it all out there. Best thing I ever did. Our relationship is booming."

My client had achieved substantial emotional growth.

Chapter 7:
Poverty and Financial Hardship

If you look at what you have in life, you'll always have more. If you look at what you don't have in life, you'll never have enough. –Oprah Winfrey

In This Chapter

Poverty is one of the greatest scourges of humankind, a chronic affliction of society. The gap between the haves and have-nots is progressively widening. However, certain actions and shifts in your thinking can bring a richness that you may not believe. So, think rich when you're poor!

The Problem of Poverty

You may be suffering from poverty, and the truth is that you're not alone. Poverty is a problem worldwide, with many places subject to much worse conditions than the developed world. Worldwide, 24% of the population, equal to 1.9 billion people, lives in impoverished conditions and dire circumstances. By far, most of these are women and children. A lack of food, shelter, clean water, and medication are severe problems, as is a lack of education (Peer, 2023). Without access to these basics, people struggle to get by from one day to the next. Many of them don't succeed.

Many in the developed world look the other way, perhaps because the extent of the suffering is too great to comprehend and too uncomfortable to face. As for myself, I sponsored a young girl in South Africa when I left school at age 18. I am fortunate to have been born in a rich country and to be enjoying peace and harmony. She wasn't. My contribution eased my conscience. For my young mind, it was a way to help narrow the inequitable situations between the haves and have-nots.

I have donated to world poverty causes for most of my life. The modest amounts I contribute each month may help me be aware of the inequities. But does it really help? I still turn away from the TV commercials relating to poverty in the developing world that show abject conditions and starvation. All too often, they're shown just as dinner is put on the table. With a more mature mind, I realize my conscience has not been eased. It's a bit like running with a blindfold on.

While the relative situations of people in poverty are less dire in developed countries, poverty is still a problem. The poverty rate in the US rose 5% from 7.4% to 12.4% during the period between 2021 and 2022. That's 38 million people. The poverty rate for children doubled from 2021 to 2022. Among older Americans, 14% were affected by poverty, despite increases in Social Security payments. Inflation and an increased cost of living, as well as the expiration of government anti-poverty programs, contributed to these numbers (Ney, 2023).

In the UK, statistics are even worse. In 2021, 1 in 5 (20%) of people lived in poverty, many of them children. Over the last 25 years, children have made up the bulk of those living in this state (Joseph Rowntree Foundation, 2023).

Australian Scientia Professor Carla Treloar, director of the Social Policy Research Center at UNSW Sydney, says "There are 3.3 million people in Australia desperately struggling to pay the bills and put food on the table. There are 761,000 children who are denied a good start to life." The Australian Council of Social Service CEO called it "a source of great shame for our nation." She added that "we can and must do better" (UNSW Sydney, 2022).

Overall, the problems of people living below the poverty line in developed countries include unemployment or inadequate wages, substandard housing, hunger, lack of access to medical care, and inflation, which sends prices for nearly everything soaring.

What's the effect of all this need? People who are struggling to survive at something approaching a greater-than-subsistence level are less able to address core issues that keep them impoverished. And their ability to pursue self-awareness and to combat the ravages of grief is crippled.

Only when they achieve a certain level of adequate income are people capable of addressing the nonmonetary problems that trouble them.

Basic Needs

The gap is progressively widening between the advantaged and disadvantaged. Poverty and financial hardship are widespread, and it can be difficult to fathom what many people must do just to survive.

The problems are quite disturbing. People in these situations can certainly feel grief over their circumstances and their inability to provide for themselves and especially their children. Understanding the reasons that these inequalities exist is also a cause for grief. How can we cope with the emotional needs of people in poverty when their physical needs aren't met?

In Chapter 3, I discussed Maslow's hierarchy of needs. At the bottom of the pyramid of needs are physiological needs and safety needs. These are exactly what those living in poverty have trouble satisfying.

Physiological needs are those that are basic to life itself: air, water, food, shelter, sleep, and clothing (some people add reproduction to the list). Safety needs are personal security, employment, resources, health, and property. In this case, property doesn't necessarily mean land but the basic ability to have personal possessions.

It's a shame that some people lack the basic physiological needs. Every day, we can see unhoused people in our cities and towns who lack adequate food and hydration. Sometimes they have tents for shelter, but in many locations, these are confiscated, and they are left with a sleeping bag—if that. Many sleep under bridges, on heating grates, in their cars, or on park benches. Others have beds in shelters, but many of these are crowded, unsanitary, and dangerous. Their clothing is seldom adequate for inclement weather.

Their safety needs are also largely unmet. Personal safety is often lacking. The unhoused are susceptible to assault, rape, and theft. Few can get jobs, or they can only sometimes get day labor. Some resources are available from the government and charities, but far fewer than can meet the need. Their health suffers from their living conditions. There is also a lack of medical care, which the impoverished usually only get from the few nonprofit hospitals and their emergency rooms. Their property consists of whatever they can carry or store in a bag or shopping cart. Many also have mental illnesses that go untreated and interfere with their ability to take care of themselves.

Other people in poverty have it slightly better. They may be able to afford a small, unsanitary apartment in a dangerous area, though, often, it's not adequate for the number of people who live there. They may live in a "food desert," an area where no grocery stores with reasonable prices exist. Or they may have to rely on food banks to supplement whatever they can afford. Much of their clothing may come from thrift shops.

Often, a family's provider must work two or even three jobs to try to make ends meet. Their healthcare largely consists of visits to the emergency room, even for common illnesses and accidents. They can't afford insurance, and the costs of emergency room visits increase their reluctance to access any healthcare unless they are desperate.

A little farther up the economic ladder are the working poor, those who may be able to rent a small house and who have a steady job. The pay from that job may not be adequate, though, especially for supporting a family. Generally, two incomes are needed, and if there is only one adult present, a child may drop out of school to go to work. The lack of education makes it less likely that they will ever find a decent job, too. Government benefits may help some people with food or income, but the amounts are seldom sufficient. Even getting to the offices to apply for assistance may be a problem because of a lack of transportation, which also makes finding and keeping a job a problem.

These days, even lower-middle-class and middle-class people and families have serious trouble making ends meet. Two incomes are almost always required, along with some government subsidies for essentials like health insurance. But these people and families are one paycheck or health crisis from falling into deeper poverty. And when a caregiver is needed for an elder or a disabled family member, their resources get stretched even thinner.

Perhaps the most troubling problem for the impoverished is the sense of not belonging and being shunned by society. Do we ignore the unhoused? Many people walk right by them. If you're in one of these situations, it's no wonder that your need for belonging is not always met. Families can break under the strain. They may find social support from churches and other organizations like 12-step groups. Neighbors often do provide what they can in the way of providing help such as childcare. But fractured families and the need to be constantly working make it almost impossible to have time or money for recreational or civic opportunities or organizational memberships where friendships can grow.

The need for esteem is next on Maslow's hierarchy, and this can be in short supply as well. Subsistence-level jobs and depressing living situations can lead to an overwhelming sense of stagnation and failure. Any setback such as a shift that you've missed because of illness, a cutback in job hours, or a raise in the rent can add to the sense of defeat.

Not all people in poverty experience this, of course. Some are able to hold their heads high and feel pride in their ability to survive despite the many challenges. The point, though, is they shouldn't have to deal with all the hardships and hazards.

At any rate, people who aren't able to meet their basic needs also aren't able to reach the goal of self-actualization. If they have emotional difficulties, which of course many do, they aren't able to find or afford help. They can and do easily suffer from anxiety, depression, and grief, which can be overwhelming and difficult to combat. It's hard to fight for your mental health when you're fighting to survive.

Finding Help

If you are suffering from financial hardship, don't be ashamed to get help wherever possible. There are many resources you can take advantage of.

Most countries have human resource centers that can address basic needs. There are government programs, both national and local, that offer help with food and nutrition, housing, and other needs (Probasco, 2023).

For example. In the US, the federal food stamp program is called the Supplemental Nutrition Assistance Program. It provides debit cards good for a certain amount of money that you can use to buy groceries. Because it's on a card, you don't stand out from all the other customers paying with bank cards.

There's also the Special Supplemental Nutrition Program for Women, Infants, and Children. It directs assistance to those who are among the most vulnerable populations. The states get federal grants that they use to provide food, healthcare referrals, and nutrition education for low-income women, infants, and children up to age five who are at nutritional risk.

Another resource is the United States Department of Agriculture National Hunger Hotline, which will provide information and eligibility requirements in English and Spanish. It will connect you with emergency food providers, government programs, and social service agencies. Other programs include the National School Lunch Program, the School Breakfast Program, and the Summer Food Service Program. They offer free or reduced-price meals for school-age children.

Seniors can also receive federal food benefits. The Senior Farmers' Market Nutrition Program offers coupons for purchasing fresh fruits, vegetables, and other products at farmers' markets, farms, and other places. The Commodity Supplemental Food Program provides healthy food every month. You must be at least 60 years old and live in an area that offers the programs to qualify for assistance.

Other federal programs offer rental, home buying, home repair, and energy efficiency assistance. You can also learn how to find emergency housing and how to avoid foreclosure and eviction, as well as how to file a complaint against a landlord. Federal and state unemployment programs provide funds to people who have no job through no fault of their own—that is to say, who haven't been fired or quit their jobs without reason.

What was previously known as "welfare" is now called Temporary Assistance for Needy Families (TANF). TANF is another federally funded, state-run benefits program designed to help families achieve independence during times of temporary hardship. Eligible recipients can receive assistance with food, housing, home energy, childcare, and job training. TANF recipients are required to participate in work activities as defined by their state.

Six major government healthcare programs provide medical or insurance help for low-income and older Americans, children, veterans, and those who have recently lost their jobs. Medicare is primarily for seniors. Medicaid and the Children's Health Insurance Program are for low-income families. They also address the needs of individuals and dependent children under 19 whose parents earn too much to qualify for Medicaid but not enough to pay for private health insurance. Both Medicaid and the Children's Health Insurance Program are partially federally funded but run at the state level. This means that each state has its own rules but must follow federal guidelines.

The Health Insurance Marketplace, created by the Affordable Care Act legislation, is designed to make affordable health insurance available to the uninsured. People whose resources are below income limits on the program can receive subsidies that help with the cost of coverage. The Consolidated Omnibus Budget Reconciliation Act is for employees and their dependents when they lose their jobs or experience a reduction in work hours that makes them ineligible for employer-sponsored insurance benefits.

The Veterans Administration's healthcare benefits are for military veterans or former members of the National Guard or Reserve who served on active duty and were honorably discharged. Eligibility does depend on when they served and for how long.

Social Security payments are another important benefits program. Social Security Disability Insurance benefits are available to people who are out of work for at least one year due to a medical condition or are expected to die from that condition. There are eligibility requirements, but you can apply online. Social Security retirement benefits provide money for seniors who are in their 60s and older. These are paid every month and are subject to a modest cost-of-living adjustment raise every year.

Federal and state programs usually have a means test or eligibility requirement that is tied to the official federal calculation of the poverty level for individuals and families. There are also state and local programs and charities that provide assistance at no or low cost. Among these are Meals on Wheels, Catholic Charities, community mental health programs, and food banks.

Many resources that offer assistance provide access to professionals who allow the needy a chance to reclaim a certain level of psychological recovery. They can be in a position to address the root causes of the financial situations that people are in.

Turn Your Life Around

Is it possible that people who live in poverty or hardship feel so displaced that they believe nobody sees them? Maybe their life is so basic and far from what is deemed normal that they believe they are not worthy. There is possibly shame and a sense of low self-worth.

There needs to be an acknowledgment of the thoughts and feelings of people who are in this situation. However, when an individual regains the ability to meet their basic needs and the determination and positive attitude to work toward change, there can be hope. There is no point in remaining angry about the services that are not provided by the government or communities where they live. There is no point in remaining bitter about the events that have led to their standard of living. Attitude is everything in establishing a mindset to start to turn your life around.

For example, instead of simply accepting your plight, you can take action to make things better. You could volunteer to put in a couple of hours working at the food bank that helps you out. You'd be paying it forward and helping others who are in the same situation. Besides, volunteer work is a good thing to put on a job application or a résumé. It shows you are a proactive self-starter and can work well with others. Or you could start a group with neighbors in your apartment building to explore solutions for the inadequacies of your residence and to organize to promote tenants' rights.

These activities will boost your confidence and promote your self-esteem. Campaigning for votes to support local or state benefits programs will give you a way to show your support for others in your situation and make a positive change for the better.

What's the meaning of the word "attitude"? It's the way you think or feel about something. Only by addressing your attitude can you start to challenge your thought processes, replace irrational thinking, and bring about change and improvement. Attitude is everything when it comes to enabling change. It can defeat both helplessness and hopelessness. You can't achieve beneficial outcomes with a negative attitude.

A positive mindset does not come from focusing on the causes and effects of hardship. In the early stages of change, your positive attitude comes when you relish the small things you experience daily and have gratitude for them. By working toward an improved outlook, you will gain the mental and emotional strength to start looking at the causes of your situation and face any associated grief.

While changing your attitude is the best possible approach to turning your life around, make sure that your basic needs are met. As I explained when discussing Maslow's hierarchy of needs, it's hard to work on your self-esteem and self-actualization if your needs for safety and security haven't been met. Advocating for yourself takes determination and courage, traits that will serve you well as you start to turn your life around. Taking advantage of available social programs is no cause for embarrassment or shame. You can take pride in the fact that you are doing everything you can to make a better life for yourself and your family. Don't buy into the belief that says such benefits are only for losers and slackers! You know the reality—that those programs are there for a reason, and that reason is helping you and other people just like you.

A Change in Mindset

To alter your attitude, your situation, and your life, you need to look within and have the determination to change. Healing from your distress and grief is difficult work; it's painful and tedious. Maybe the hill seems too great to climb; maybe you are in shock or denial of what has happened or is happening in your life. You need to allow whatever time is required to nurture your mind and work on yourself and your attitude. Then, whenever possible, seek a mental health professional who can guide you through the processes. Remember that there are free or low-cost services available to help you work through life issues. Section 3 of this book offers suggestions that can be part of a mental health recovery plan.

Healing is not about acquiring material items, money, or wealth. It depends on finding pleasure in and gratitude for simple things in life. Wealth is never the size of your wallet—it comes from the heart. It's a mindset that can be overlooked by people who are more fortunate in their material situation. If you have a real appreciation of and gratitude for what you do have and not just a focus on what you don't have, your mind will be well-prepared for grief work that will address the root causes of the situation you are in—if you realize there is a need for change.

Perception and perspective are what really matter in life. Sometimes you need to experience hard living, have it thrown in your face, or "take one on the chin." Once this happens, you gain (or at least strive for) the right attitude; once you have gratitude for what you have, watch what happens. Mentally, the gap narrows between the haves and have-nots. When you reach this point, you have renewed emotional energy. Maybe the urgency has lessened. With the right mindset, rational thinking, and understanding, you are now able to make priority decisions for your future.

Think rich when you're poor. Embrace appreciation and gratitude. See what happens when you change your perspective!

My Stories

If you are poor or unhoused, remember that there are many people who care about your situation. They don't judge. They just want you to know they care.

One year, one of my sisters and I wanted to do something meaningful for the unhoused in one of our big cities. On Christmas Eve we bought hundreds of dollars' worth of McDonald's burgers and Christmas stockings. It was kind of a peculiar combination, but that was what we came up with. We kept driving our car around the city center, and each time we stopped, we grabbed one of the bags from the back seat. Then, we walked the footpaths looking for unhoused people to give the bags to. When they received a burger and a Christmas stocking, the surprise and sheer gratitude of the recipients were nearly overwhelming.

At one of our last stops at the subway station, we saw a disheveled man with two young children sitting on a bench. The look of desperation in their eyes was heartbreaking. We wished them a merry Christmas and told them we were thinking of them. We gave them each a burger and a Christmas stocking. The absolute delight on their faces is something I have never forgotten. Turning to his children, the father said, "See, I told you: There are good people in this world." Then, he hugged us.

Thankfully, the stairs to the street were only a few yards away because, as we went in that direction, my sister and I looked at each other. We both had tears streaming down our faces.

***

Materialism can be just a deficiency in realism. Ask yourself: What is really important in life?

For two years, I lived in a wealthy suburb. Then, I moved to one of the poorer socioeconomic areas of the city. At the time, I was living away from my partner. She was concerned for my welfare, but I told her not to be worried.

I have spoken to many of my family members about this experience and the revelation I had.

It was refreshing and uplifting each time I went down to the shopping center. Before, when I shopped in the rich suburb, it felt so impersonal and rushed, with a real sense of being apart from others. This feeling had not been apparent until I moved. When I shopped in the poorer neighborhood, I noticed something special.

There were two situations I particularly noticed. One was the number of young teens happily shopping with their moms and dads. They weren't wandering around the shopping center. They were happy to just be with their parents. I also noticed how beautifully most of the parents spoke to their toddlers. I loved it, but I did not try and make any sense of it at first; I just enjoyed my shopping trips.

Over time, I realized the reason for it. Shopping was a family event. The shopping trip was probably a big event for those teenagers, a fun outing that they did not experience often. Perhaps they did not have all the material goods that others may have had. Those kids seemed so content. Those parents seemed to relish their youngsters because that is all that mattered to them. They may not have had many material things in life, but one thing is for certain—they sure loved, respected, and cherished their children. They showed gratitude with every word they spoke. It was refreshing to observe the perspective they had.

***

I have the richest parents in the world.

In my childhood, we lived in some very modest circumstances. My parents chose to live simply, without too many creature comforts, so that they could guarantee we had the best opportunities in life. They worked several jobs each so they could have us educated in a private high school. My siblings and I never felt we were missing out on anything. There was always good food on the table and plenty of entertainment outside. We made our own fun. There was always much love and happiness. We loved our childhood and teenage years.

We never realized how hard it was for our parents until we became adults and heard the stories of how they struggled. One day, about 15 years ago, I was sitting out back with my dad when he became quite upset.

He said, "My biggest regret in life is not being able to leave you much when I am gone."

I was taken aback by this disclosure. My reply was, "But you have given us everything, Dad."

I went on to say, "Wealth is not the size of your wallet; it is the size of your heart. It comes from the heart, Dad. What you have given makes me feel so bloody rich. I never forget that."

He appreciated that emotional comfort, but what I said wasn't just words—I truly meant it. In my eyes, he's 10 feet tall and the richest man I know.

What's Next?

If you recognized yourself in the previous four chapters, you're not alone. Both the causes and effects of grief happen to lots of people every day. But what can you do about grief? Isn't it just something you have to get through by simply waiting for it to pass?

The answer is no! You don't have to continue suffering the ravages of grief without any help. Professional mental health practitioners can guide you through types of therapy that they can facilitate, as well as techniques you can do on your own that will lessen the sting. With the right kind of help, you can learn ways to renew your life, your satisfaction, and even your happiness.

When you find a new lease on life, you'll have escaped from the hold that grief has had on you. You'll become your own best friend and have the tools to face grief if you should experience adverse life events in the future.

Your brain, your emotions, and your life will be transformed!

Section 3:

Create Positive Change

Chapter 8:
Techniques and Psychology

What I love about therapy is that they'll tell you what your blind spots are. Although that's uncomfortable and painful, it gives you something to work with. –
Pink

In This Chapter

Do you want to find ways to change your life? We've looked at some major life issues that can be extremely difficult to navigate through to achieve some sort of normality. Now, we'll look at skills and techniques that can become effective life skills, which are a natural way to process information in the future. Emotional awareness, once you've mastered and applied it, fosters emotional growth.

Basic Psychology

Psychology is the study of the human mind and its functions, especially those affecting emotions and behavior. Psychotherapy offers techniques designed to change thinking patterns and improve coping skills. While this is easy in theory, it can be difficult to experience and incorporate into your life. However, psychological therapy can be life-changing when you are engaged and committed to the process.

Psychological theory has developed a lot in the years since it was pioneered by Sigmund Freud. He started the practice called psychoanalysis, which explores unconscious and repressed memories and feelings through techniques like dream analysis and free association. It's a process that can take years.

Nowadays, mental health practitioners are more likely to provide short-term therapies that aim to develop a client's coping skills and understanding of their condition. There are many competing theories and approaches that practitioners have tried and found helpful for a variety of problems. The *Diagnostic and Statistical Manual of Mental Disorders* aids psychiatrists and therapists in determining what their clients are experiencing—mood disorders like anxiety, depression, and grief, for example, or more serious problems like schizophrenia.

In writing this book, I've focused on mood disorders, which are more likely to respond to therapies that can be accomplished with the help of a professional or alleviated by practices that you can do on your own.

Different Kinds of Grief

There is not just one style of grief. It's very personal and differs for different people. Some people suffer in silence, for example, while others express themselves with great displays of feeling. There's nothing wrong with either of these grief styles. They depend on a person's nature and personality, their upbringing, and how they experience difficult emotions.

If a child sees their parents responding to grief with a stoic, stiff-upper-lip attitude, they may get the message that this is the proper way to grieve. If another child sees parents respond with extreme outward signs of sorrow, they may think that *that* is the proper way to respond. If different family members display a variety of different responses to loss, the child may become confused about the "right" way to grieve, not realizing that there isn't just one.

Knowing that other people also experience grief in different ways doesn't make it easier when it's you who's going through it. Your grief is personal to you because you have different memories of what caused your loss. If a friend or a person close to your family dies, you'll have different memories and experiences of that person than anyone else will. You'll all have processed those memories in different ways.

And if your grief isn't caused by a death—say it was your business failing that has caused it—no one close to you may have experienced the same sort of trauma or have any context for your loss. They may not understand at all.

When it comes to different ways of approaching grief, the American Psychological Association defines "normal" grief as lasting from six months to two years. It doesn't interfere with your daily activities (Moberly, 2021). If it doesn't fit into those guidelines exactly, that doesn't mean that what you're feeling isn't real grief.

Here's a look at different kinds of grief and how you may experience them.

Anticipatory grief affects you when you know that a loss is coming. For example, a businessperson may know their business is failing months before it actually collapses. Knowing that a divorce is imminent is another example. All the same, it's still grief and just as valid and understandable as grief after a traumatic event such as a death.

Delayed grief, on the other hand, doesn't hit immediately after a loss. Maybe you have too many other responsibilities that prevent you from expressing your emotions fully until those details are taken care of. If you grew up in a culture that discourages open displays of grief, you may not realize that you have to go through a process of grieving. It may hit you later when you're not expecting it.

Cumulative grief happens when you experience several losses in a relatively short period of time. For example, if your spouse divorces you soon after your business fails, you'll experience those causes for grief virtually on top of one another. One of the losses may seem to be less significant, and you may not realize that you need to grieve both.

Disenfranchised grief occurs when those around you, like your family or your culture, don't recognize that you have a sufficient cause for grief. Many people, for example, don't understand how deeply the death of a pet can affect its owner. They may say, "It's just a cat" and invalidate the very real loss a person experiences. In essence, other people are telling them that they have no right to grieve.

There are also different styles for processing grief. Intuitive grievers, for example, are more likely to let their emotions show in open displays. They find it easier than other grieving people to look for or accept help such as therapy or a support group. Instrumental grievers are more likely to channel their grief into action, for example by starting or giving to a charity in honor of the deceased or to help victims of crime.

But grieving is a continuum. Few people are wholly at either end of the spectrum when it comes to the process. Most are blended grievers, who embrace both styles of grieving to one extent or another.

The important thing to remember is that your grief is your own. No one can tell you that you're doing it wrong, or you shouldn't listen to them if they do. If you grieve for longer than they feel is appropriate, you're not wallowing. If your grieving doesn't last as long as others expect it to, you aren't being cold or unfeeling. You're grieving in your own way, in your own time, according to how you feel the loss. Know that it's valid.

When You Have a Problem

The first step to resolving a problem is admitting that you have one. You may be reluctant to do this, but it's necessary if you want to heal. In general, you need help if your emotions and behavior interfere with your daily life and normal functions. For example, you may find yourself experiencing difficulty with your work life or love life, or simply being unable to sleep at night or get out of bed in the morning. In extreme cases, you can even find yourself with more serious problems that can cause major disruptions in your life, like overspending or reckless driving.

The second step in dealing with your difficulties is making a commitment to address your problems and exploring your emotions, thoughts, and behavior. You need to have the determination to follow through with therapeutic practices and techniques you can try that will help you achieve your goals.

What you discover about yourself and your past behavior can be very difficult, upsetting, or stressful. You're challenging your thought processes and some of the concepts that you've believed for a long time. It can be very distressing to address the root causes of problems that may stem from things that happened to you when you were a child. Rest assured that the results are worth it. When you experience freedom from your troubles, you can get back to the way you want to live your life.

Strategies That Can Help

There are several techniques that you can practice without the aid of a mental health professional. Some of them come from practices such as yoga, which may also prove beneficial. These practices concentrate on controlling your bodily reactions and your emotional state.

Many people consider yoga, tai chi, and other similar practices to be mere fads or even religious rituals. In reality, they are harmless and even beneficial, and they can be practiced regardless of religion. Try them and see what effects they have on your mood and thoughts.

For now, we'll explore controlled breathing and mindfulness. Then, we'll take a look at concepts that therapists often use with their clients to assist them in addressing their problems.

Controlled Breathing

When you are upset, your breathing changes. If you have anxiety or fear, for instance, your breathing is likely to speed up. You could even experience light-headedness because rapid, shallow breathing doesn't provide sufficient oxygen to your brain. On the other hand, if you have fear regarding something that you think is about to happen, you may find yourself holding your breath, which also doesn't provide enough oxygen to allow you to think clearly.

Studies have shown that slowing your breathing increases "comfort, relaxation, pleasantness, vigor, and alertness" and reduces "symptoms of arousal, anxiety, depression, anger, and confusion." There is also evidence that controlled breathing is "related to emotional control and psychological well-being" (Zaccaro et al., 2018). The key is concentrating on the breath alone. Clear your mind and control your breathing.

The general aim of controlling your breathing is to shift from breathing with your upper chest to breathing with your abdomen. Sit comfortably and upright to raise your rib cage and expand your chest. Or lie down if you prefer. Place one hand on your chest, and the other on your abdomen so you notice how your upper chest and abdomen are moving while you are breathing. Concentrate on your breath and try to breathe in and out gently through your nose. Feel your breath as you inhale and exhale. If you're able to, try to practice upper-chest breathing when you become upset.

One of the simplest breathing exercises is called "box breathing." You do it by imagining a box with its four sides in front of you. Draw in a breath and count to four as you think about the top side of the box. Keep your lungs full for four more seconds as you think about the second side. Then, exhale for four seconds as you visualize the third side of the box. Finally, hold that state of breathing for a count of four as you think about the last side of the box.

You can repeat this exercise a few times at the start and increase the number of repetitions as you become used to it. Try practicing it 10 to 20 times in a session once you are ready. The key is concentrating on your breath alone. Clear your mind and control the flow of air. You can also try it in bed if you have trouble sleeping.

Alternate nostril breathing is another easy-to-practice breathing exercise. To do it, sit comfortably. Breathe regularly at first. After you exhale, use one of your thumbs to close the same-side nostril. Inhale through your other nostril. Then, use your pointer finger to close that nostril and take a breath through the other one. Exhale through that nostril. That's one repetition. Keep doing this for up to five minutes.

Mindfulness

Mindfulness is a form of meditation that focuses your attention on your senses instead of your thoughts or emotions. It shifts your attention and directs it to the present moment rather than remaining worried about the past or the future. You move your attention away from what is distressing you and refocus it on what's around you. Your brain follows wherever your attention is.

As you practice mindfulness, you can feel calmer, be more able to deal with difficult thoughts, and improve your concentration. It's been found to lessen anxiety and depression, improve sleep, and lower blood pressure. You learn to pay attention to your body's signals and to respond to them with healthful practices. You can find plenty of mindfulness exercises and advice online, or you can explore mindfulness yourself with these simple ideas.

You can start by examining your surroundings using your five senses. First, notice the sensations associated with your breathing or try one of the above breathing exercises. Then, notice what you can see, hear, smell, touch, and taste. Perhaps you can see the sun shining through a window and feel the warmth of it on your skin. You could smell the scent of the chili cooking on the stove and hear the water running as you wash your hands. Maybe you can still taste the onion and hot peppers from when you sampled the chili while you were preparing it.

You can also do a mindfulness exercise by concentrating your attention on a single piece of fruit. Make it something that you can easily hold in your mouth, like a raspberry. Pick up the raspberry and feel its texture in your fingers. Lift it to your nose and inhale its scent. Then, pop it in your mouth, but don't eat it yet. Roll the berry around on your tongue. Can you feel the slight prickles on your tongue? Now bite into it. Feel the sensation of the juice filling your mouth. Does the taste change? Savor all the sensations associated with the fruit.

You can do mindfulness exercises anywhere and at any time. If you're at the office and feeling tense, for example, take note of one thing you can see, hear, smell, touch, and taste. Or go sit in your car and notice the sensations there. Maybe you're chewing gum or sucking on a breath mint, so you have something to taste. Maybe you can still taste what you had for lunch.

Another type of mindfulness activity is the body scan. You can do it while sitting, standing, or lying down, indoors or outdoors—wherever, whenever, and however it feels best to you. It takes about five minutes. Close your eyes or leave them half open but focused on nothing in particular. Take a few deep breaths, inhaling oxygen and allowing yourself to relax. Notice the sensations of your feet on the floor or your body on the bed or mat. Notice your legs, the pressure of them.

Do they feel heavy or light? Then, notice the sensations in your back. Is it relaxed or tense? Does it hurt at all?

Next, focus on your stomach area. If it feels tense, can you relax it? Remember to breathe from your abdomen. Then, direct your attention to your hands and arms. If they are taut or tight, try to relax them. One way to do this is to purposely contract them up as much as you can and then release all the tension. Then, notice your neck and how it feels. Shift your attention to your face. Notice if your jaw is clenched. Let your facial muscles relax.

Finally, take a deep breath and notice what your whole body is feeling. Open your eyes, but again, don't focus them on anything. Gently rotate your neck and head; then, open your eyes fully and take in your surroundings. When you feel ready, stand up and return to your normal breathing.

Cognitive Behavioral Therapy

Cognitive behavioral therapy (CBT) is a therapeutic psychological technique that is quite popular now. It was first developed in the 1960s when American psychiatrist Aaron Beck "began to notice that his patients with depression often verbalized thoughts that were lacking in validity and noted characteristic 'cognitive distortions' in their thinking" (Chand, et al., 2022). He proposed that anxiety, depression, and other disorders such as eating disorders, anger issues, insomnia, and phobias were based on incorrect or unproductive thoughts, feelings, and behaviors. CBT was designed to challenge these beliefs and replace them with more beneficial ones. It has been studied and found to be as effective as other forms of therapy and psychiatric medication, though medication can also be a part of the treatment (Chand, et al., 2022).

The three basic principles of CBT are that, in part, psychological problems are based on faulty thinking, that the problems can be partly attributed to unhealthy ways of behaving that are often learned patterns, and that you can learn better ways of coping with your problems. CBT sets out to allow you to recognize what these faulty thoughts and behaviors are; to develop coping strategies and the confidence in yourself to overcome your unhelpful thoughts; and to learn coping skills that will help you deal with problematic situations and people.

Facing and changing your behaviors rather than avoiding the causes are important techniques. Role-playing and relaxation can play a part in this process. The goal is to equip you with the ability to apply these strategies for yourself without depending on the therapist. There are many videos and workbooks that you may find helpful in this process, but to be successful, a therapist is essential at the beginning to teach you how to recognize and change your faulty thoughts and unhelpful behaviors.

You and the therapist work together to accomplish your goals. The mental health practitioner adapts the sessions to address your specific situation. For example, they may give you homework—exercises for you to do that are relevant to what you are experiencing.

Rather than examining your past life, CBT focuses on the current problems you are having. Of course, a certain amount of knowledge of your history is needed to understand how and why you developed faulty thought and behavior patterns. But, unlike psychoanalysis, this does not make up most of the session or take a great deal of time. CBT instead emphasizes how you will think and act in the future.

Some of the kinds of faulty thinking include

- black-and-white thinking, which is an all-or-nothing attitude that does not allow for shades of gray

- overgeneralization, where someone takes a single event and believes it applies to every situation

- selective thinking, or focusing on one aspect of a situation instead of the whole thing

- ignoring the positive and focusing solely on the bad parts of what has happened

- mind-reading, which involves a person thinking they know what another person is thinking

- fortune-telling, which is when a person believes they know how a situation will turn out

- catastrophizing, or always believing that the worst is going to happen

- blame, or thinking that you (or another person) are responsible for all bad situations and results

These kinds of faulty thinking arise from assumptions about yourself, other people, and how the world works. For example, you may believe that you are unlovable. This can lead to the behavior of always trying to please other people. This can grow into never pleasing yourself and feeling depressed because you never get what you desire. Or, if you believe that people are out to get you, you may think that you have to avoid other people as much as possible. You may develop anxiety about being in social situations.

One thing that is important to know about CBT is that it can be quite difficult. It's not easy to challenge your thoughts, core beliefs, and behavior. And just becoming aware of unhealthy and destructive thought patterns is very different from actually changing them. Time and effort are required, and you must be committed to the process. Even though CBT is often considered a short-term form of therapy, progress can be slow and gradual. Don't expect instant results. The techniques I just discussed—controlled breathing and mindfulness—are often part of the treatment, too.

Dialectic behavioral theory (DBT) is a form of therapy that is related to CBT. "Dialectical" refers to taking two opposites and integrating them. It was first developed to treat personality disorders but has also proved effective in addressing anxiety and depression. The principles are to accept things the way they are and to make changes that improve what you're experiencing. In addition to individual therapy, DBT can include group therapy regarding developing coping skills and phone coaching with a therapist during crisis situations.

Narrative Therapy

Narrative therapy is often used in conjunction with CBD to separate you from your problems and see them as external to you rather than internal. Acceptance and dignity are key to narrative therapy. It emphasizes seeing yourself not as a bad person but as a person who has made mistakes. You and your therapist can use narrative techniques to address anxiety, depression, anger, emotional regulation, and different kinds of trauma.

You're the expert on your own life. A therapist will often need to learn more about you and encourage you to provide stories about your life. Some of these stories are more relevant to your problems than others.

The therapist will separate you from your problem and discuss times and situations throughout your life to identify your values and belief systems. This is important for them to get a viewpoint from your frame of reference and to allow them to trace the history and effects of a problem to uncover positive outcomes. Your dreams, values, goals, and skills are what make up your reality.

A few of the main principles of narrative therapy are that interactions with other people create reality and that an understandable story helps you organize yours. These stories help you understand what happens and has happened to you. It's how you make meaning out of your experiences. Then, you explore alternative stories that help you "rewrite" your experience to make a new one that's not tied to your previous experience of your life and difficulties. The new narrative can explain and define a different reality.

There's not just one new narrative that you can create, though. You can imagine several alternative realities that you could incorporate into your new life. You can select stories that have better outcomes and work to make them a reality.

If you decide that narrative therapy is for you, you need to find a mental health professional who has been trained in the technique and who is someone that you feel comfortable with. Revealing your stories may sometimes be painful and rewriting them may be difficult. You can interview potential therapists before you select one and check their credentials to determine whether you can work with them successfully. Many therapists will let you ask pre-appointment questions over a video call or on the phone.

Distraction Techniques

Often, in CBT, a therapist will use distraction techniques to give you a break from the distress of the therapy process. Distractions can enable you to focus on something pleasant or neutral to defuse an episode of increasing anxiety, for example. You could try a few minutes of the breathing techniques mentioned above. Other means of distraction include thinking of a pleasant memory to give yourself a hit of pleasure or reciting the alphabet backward to give your mind something else to focus on. The key is to recharge but not to use distraction techniques as a way to avoid the pain of self-discovery. It's important not to think of temporary avoidance as a solution to your problems. That's a way to give yourself some short-term relief but not long-term success.

CBT distraction techniques such as imagining your perfect vacation can be cathartic, as many psychological treatments and therapies are. Catharsis means a powerful emotional release, and it can be an important part of the healing process. You may become quite emotional at the thought of a pleasant memory. There may be root causes that release a great deal of distress. If an environment feels safe and you have confidence in and comfort with the therapist, then success in the entire process is more likely. This is another important reason for professional guidance and being satisfied with your choice of a therapist to work through psychological issues with.

Acceptance and Commitment Therapy

By using acceptance and commitment therapy (ACT), you learn not to avoid or deny the emotions you are experiencing. That's the acceptance part of the therapy. Instead, you view your feelings as natural states that help you commit to moving ahead. You learn that your emotions are appropriate reactions to your situation. For example, if you have just been through a traumatic divorce, your emotions may include sadness, anger, or guilt, to name a few.

Acceptance means that you understand that these emotions are valid and not to be discounted or repressed. What we often consider negative emotions like sadness, disappointment, or anger are actually valid and even appropriate reactions to your circumstances.

Among the principles of ACT are observing a thought without judging it, recognizing that you are more than your thoughts, feelings, and reactions, and living according to your personal values rather than trying to avoid distress or abide by other people's expectations.

Next comes the commitment part of ACT. You take concrete steps in order to make positive changes that will align with your values. Among the techniques are recognizing difficult thoughts or situations and developing skills that will enable you to make changes in your life. Mindfulness and commitment to change are important features of the therapy.

Self-Talk

Self-talk is made up of the messages that you give yourself throughout an ordinary day. It's like an inner voice that narrates your experience. Many people think that their inner voice means their conscience, something inside them that tells them what is good and bad, moral or immoral. But self-talk is not like that at all.

If you have thoughts like *I forgot to pick up eggs at the grocery store today*, that's normal and not harmful. But if you think *I always forget things. I'm totally useless*, you are telling yourself something that will lower your self-esteem and make you feel bad about yourself. If you do this often enough, you'll start believing it. It will become part of your core beliefs and affect the way you think about yourself.

I have a friend who constantly says how dumb he is. I always correct him and say, "You are not dumb, mate. Stop saying that."

He might then rephrase his criticism of what he has just done. He begins changing his self-talk.

Changing your self-talk is as important as CBT is in dealing with grief and adverse life events. This is a time when retraining your brain is exactly what you need. When you develop rational thinking and continually train your brain to make that thinking part of your self-talk, you will have taken a giant step toward healing.

My empathy is something I pride myself on. Empathy means having the ability to understand the experiences and feelings of others, outside of your own perspective. When I start to cast judgment or have preconceived ideas, I automatically say to myself with my inner voice, "What they're saying or doing is from their frame of reference" or "Don't assume."

If you make it a daily practice to correct your inner voice, you'll be honing it. Keep thinking of your mind as a magnificent computer. Why would you want to put bullshit talk into your personal database? This is only a virus.

But how can you retrain your brain to tell you what you need to hear in order to build you up rather than tear you down? Two of the most effective methods are thought-stopping and thought replacement.

First, you need to identify your negative thoughts. Keep a diary of the irrational thoughts you have over the course of one day. You could also use a pocket recorder to make a recording on the spot. Write down your inner criticisms at the end of the day.

When you become adept at recognizing your irrational or unproductive thoughts, you're ready to begin thought-stopping. It's literally what it says. When you "hear" yourself criticizing yourself unfairly, tell your brain to stop. You can tell yourself this using your inner voice (especially if you're out in public). Or you can actually do the thought-stopping out loud. Simply think or say, "No!" or "Stop!"

Next, you learn thought replacement. Take that diary or list of negative or irrational thoughts you made and think of something you could tell yourself instead of the inner insult. For example, you could say, "I forgot the eggs, but I remembered everything else we needed," "I don't always forget things. Everyone forgets things at times. It's normal," or "I'm not useless. There are many things I do well."

Write the new thought next to the irrational thought on your list. Read it over first thing in the morning and remind yourself to replace any negative thoughts you stop during the day. Make it a habit.

Journaling

Your list of stopped thoughts and replacement thoughts can easily turn into a journal. You don't have to buy a special book to use as a diary. You can use a legal pad or start a file on your computer. You can even dictate your thoughts into a recorder and have an audio journal. However, having a written journal is better for going back and finding a section you want to revisit.

The written word is powerful. One reason is that you are using several of your senses. You see what you are writing. You feel the pen in your hand or your fingers on the keyboard. You are writing down sensations, emotions, thoughts, feelings, and behaviors. Journaling can be done for your use only, but it can also be a great way to record information that you want to discuss with your mental health professional—a review of your mental status and behavior.

If you write in your journal every night, read it over the next morning. Remind yourself of how you felt and what you thought and did. Use this as data to program your supercomputer for the rest of the day. Alternatively, write in your journal only when you feel you have something important to record. It's your journal. You can use it any way you choose.

When I was healing from depression, I made it a ritual each night to write down my experiences from the day. When I was having a difficult emotional moment, I would write it down. I soon was able to correct my thoughts and feelings, which in turn brought about a desired behavior, all from just writing the experience down.

Affirmations

You may have heard of affirmations. They're positive statements that people use to reinforce themselves for their good qualities. They're a lot like replacement thoughts, except that you use them every day, not just when you have a negative thought. The goal is to train your subconscious mind to think in terms of what you already are and what you can do.

Affirmations have come in for their share of criticism. Some people find that affirmations set too high a bar for a person to achieve. "Every day in every way, I am getting better and better" is, after all, a pretty big sentiment for someone who is suffering from depression to believe. Other people find them sappy and doubt their effectiveness. But millions of people have taken up the process and see beneficial effects.

You may want to start simply, with general statements: "I'm a good person," "I am worthy," or "I love myself." Then, you can think of more specific good things to reinforce about yourself: "I am a good friend," "I can do many things well," or "I am thoughtful and kind."

Repeat these affirmations to yourself every day. You can write them on the first page of your journal and start the morning with them. Many people write affirming statements on sticky notes and place them around their bathroom mirror. If you do that, you'll see them first thing every morning and last thing at night. You can even find a Bible verse or saying that inspires you and recite it to yourself every morning or evening.

Ensure your mind is clear and thinking of nothing but the words you are writing or saying. I have been doing this practice for years and swear by it for creating a real positive mental attitude to start my day. Some people stick with the same affirmations every day, but others change them as they feel inspired to. Feel a sense of conviction and positivity that this is what you think about yourself right now.

Don't forget to reinforce yourself for your positive behaviors as well:

"I listened when Mary Jo needed to talk. I have empathy."

"I completed the project that was due today. I am a good worker."

"I remembered to buy my wife flowers for her birthday. I'm a thoughtful husband."

The author Dr. David Hamilton (2022) reports, "Scientists have discovered that when people write self-affirmations, they tend to subsequently make positive, healthy, life choices and even feel a stronger, larger sense of self." He also says, "University of Pennsylvania researchers showed that repeating self-affirmations produces physical changes in brain regions associated with self-processing, ultimately impacting their view of themselves, and these changes are associated with subsequent positive changes in people's behavior." That's a pretty big endorsement and a reason to give affirmations a try.

You may like to research more about affirmations or discuss them with mental health professionals. In theory, they are quite simple, but they do require repetition to become second nature.

Art Therapy

Creativity can bring you out of your own head and into the world. There are therapists who know how to direct art therapy or start art therapy groups. You can also do art therapy on your own. "Art therapy uses creativity to promote healing and help you process your grief. It can support, improve, and restore functioning and a sense of well-being ... [It's] the belief that artistic and creative self-expression can have a healing effect on us" (Kelly, 2021).

The artistic movement known as Abstract Expressionism is a particularly fruitful one to explore. Abstract Expressionism began in the 1940s and 1950s as a kind of stream-of-consciousness method of approaching feelings. It grew out of stream-of-consciousness writing, which is another technique you can try.

This therapy practice taps into the subconscious mind to express feelings through art. You don't ignore your grief, but you express it in the act of creating something meaningful to you. Art is a tool to unlock your emotions. It's about the process rather than the product. You take your emotions and express them in a safe space.

Art therapy can use many different materials depending on what you're drawn to. Painting and drawing are the media that are most often used, but sculpting, making collages, and even coloring or paint-by-numbers are options. You don't have to create a formal oil painting. You can use watercolor, acrylic, charcoal, pastels, or photography as a medium for expressing your emotions. Your state of mind directs how you apply them.

Art therapy doesn't have to mean the visual arts. Writing stories, songs, or poetry is also a kind of art. These can be planned, stream-of-consciousness, or a response to a prompt. Singing is also a way to express your feelings, even if you aren't a trained singer. Making and listening to a playlist of songs or instrumentals that have special meaning for you can also be cathartic.

And if you really want to tap into both sides of your brain, try painting or drawing with both hands at once. Just because the right hemisphere of the brain is said to be more creative doesn't mean that your logical side can't bring you insights as well.

If you are committed to your self-improvement and emotional awareness and become familiar with the principles suggested in this chapter, there is a very good chance to reduce or eliminate distorted thought processes and unhelpful feelings and behavior. This knowledge will complement the treatment you receive from your mental health practitioner. Once you master the techniques, you will go from emotional awareness to substantial emotional growth.

Chapter 9:
Commit, Apply, Revive

There is no normal life that is free of pain. It's the very wrestling with our problems that can be the impetus for our growth. –Fred Rogers

In This Chapter

Healing takes time and requires patience. It's not unusual to fall back into old habits or irrational thinking. Stay committed to your recovery and have confidence in the process.

Grief and Psychotherapy

Throughout this book, I've been emphasizing how psychotherapy can help you work through the grief that comes from major life events such as divorce, estrangement, poverty, and financial hardship. Of course, there are techniques you can use, such as controlled breathing, mindfulness, journaling, and affirmations that will help you, but there is no substitute for professional help. A mental health practitioner can help you determine what is causing your grief, and they can teach you methods of coping with it and healing from it. They can work with you using CBT or other effective methods to lessen your anxiety or depression.

Therapy with a professional practitioner can help you explore cultural and societal factors, such as your heritage and socioeconomic status, that influence the grieving process. With a therapist or another counselor, you can receive guidance and support. A mental health practitioner can also put you in touch with support groups and therapy groups that can help you process grief and find healing.

Grieving is important. You have every right to grieve when hardships disrupt your life. Expressing your grief is important, too. It helps you start to get relief. The emotions you need to express may include shock, disbelief, anger, and bargaining. There could also be resentment, spite, hate, or regret. You'll need to work through all of these emotions. That's where healing begins. Your therapist will help you resolve these emotions. Then, they will help you challenge the negative thought processes that caused you to suppress your emotions. Your therapist will make sure that you grieve as you need to so that you can begin to get relief.

Both grief and adverse life events affect your relationships. You may be having trouble navigating these complexities, and therapy can enhance your skills to deal with interpersonal dynamics.

Resilience is another aspect of dealing with your particular situation that therapy can help with. Resilience means that you are able to bounce back from your suffering and return to your normal life. A counselor can help you develop the skills that will support this ability. In the end, grieving will become your solace. When you begin to grieve effectively, your momentum toward recovery increases.

You and Your Therapist

Counseling is a privilege, and most professional therapists recognize this. Choosing a therapist who you can trust and work with is one of the most important decisions you'll make. You need one that you can click with. You have a unique personality and so do healthcare professionals. If you and your therapist don't communicate well with each other, there's less chance that they'll be able to help you. If you're able to engage with them, you'll make better progress. Therapy is an active process, so you need to show that you have the courage and commitment to do the necessary work.

Sharing with your therapist is the essence of the relationship. But your therapist won't share much, if any, of their life or feelings. Don't feel insulted or think that they are withholding something about your treatment. A therapist has to keep some distance between themselves and their clients. If they don't, they may become too involved with your problems and not be able to help their other clients. Therefore, they must maintain a professional boundary.

As you progress with therapy, what you need from your therapist may change. At first, you may need someone nondirective who will simply listen to you and encourage you to talk with gentle questions. Later in your healing, you could need someone who will help you challenge your assumptions so that you can come to comprehend the root causes of your grief and other emotions.

You may need a therapist who will give you homework assignments that you can complete at home and then bring to your next session to discuss. Doing the homework is important. A one-hour session a week isn't all that it will take to relieve your pain. Completing assignments will show that you have the motivation to do the necessary work. It helps you both keep track of your symptoms and how close you are to achieving your goals.

As the professional relationship with your therapist grows, what happens in the sessions will, too. At first, you'll reveal what is causing you pain. Then, you'll uncover what you want to do about it. Maybe you want to erase your pain altogether. But that may not be practical or possible. It's more realistic to try to achieve enough stability to live with what has happened to cause your psychological difficulties. Later, you can work on strategies to help alleviate your symptoms.

If something your therapist suggests doesn't work for you, don't be shy about telling them. A treatment plan is like a roadmap that your therapist creates when you first start working together. They need to know how well it's working or whether they need to tweak or change it.

As you progress through therapy, you may experience unwelcome emotions such as despair or rage. You may even feel angry with your therapist. These are actually signs that you are making progress with your therapy. You are getting in touch with long-buried emotions, even if you're directing them at the wrong person.

Eventually, you will come to the end of what the therapeutic relationship can do for you. If you have experienced relief from your symptoms and can comprehend the powerful emotions that caused them, you may be ready to go it alone. Talk it over with your therapist. They'll be honest if they think you still have more work to do. Or they may agree with you that the treatment plan has proved effective.

After you stop seeing your therapist, you can still contact them if you have a relapse of your symptoms. A booster treatment may be needed. Keep their contact information where you can find it.

Root Causes of Grief

Sometimes the root causes of your grief can be suppressed or obscured by what has happened to you in the time since—or even before—the traumatic event in your life occurred. Your irrational thoughts and beliefs may arise from something that happened to you in childhood, for example. Or you may have basic beliefs about yourself and the world that color your way of thinking.

You may feel angry at yourself or embarrassed when you realize you've been suppressing these emotions or how much they've been influencing your current thinking and behavior. Remember Samantha, the woman I talked about in Chapter 4 on anxiety? Her social anxiety disorder was deep-rooted. She spent nearly a decade trying to cope with her disorder before she sought the necessary help to get on the path to recovery. She was livid with herself when she realized how blatantly obvious the causes of her problem were and how she had continued living a life of misery before she got help for it. Until she recognized the roots and released her suppressed emotions, she couldn't approach healing.

The strategies and techniques I shared in Chapter 8 can cause your suppressed emotions to rise to the surface. Some of the techniques you can do by yourself, while others, such as CBT, require the assistance of a mental health professional. If you need medication to relieve the anxiety or depression you're feeling, you definitely need to find a therapist who can recommend a psychiatrist or nurse practitioner to give you a prescription. If you can't find one in your area or have to wait a long time to get an appointment, your family doctor may be able to prescribe medication for you in the meantime.

Identifying the causes of your unproductive emotions and learning to heal from them can be liberating, shocking, or a combination of both. But bringing them to your conscious mind and releasing them from their hidden state is ultimately a precursor to healing. Once you comprehend how your distorted thoughts and beliefs have affected you, you can begin retraining your brain so that they don't cause you emotional distress. You'll then be well on your way to recovery.

It's time to focus on the present and your new life skills. It's time to let go of self-blame and guilt. You may have had a knowledge base that was built solely in the past. Now, it's time to move on and have positivity and optimism for the future. When you achieve this, your life will turn around.

Setbacks

Along the way, however, it's not unusual to experience setbacks. You've been living with your pain and grief for a long time. Resolving them will take time. You can't just flick a switch and expect your brain to change. Reprogramming it is a process that can't be rushed. It doesn't just happen overnight. After all, you've been developing your database from the moment of your birth. A therapist can help you shorten the process, but they can't just make your emotions and feelings disappear. That takes work on your part, too.

The beliefs you need to change are likely to be deeply entrenched and challenging them can't be done in the blink of an eye. Just identifying them takes time; changing them needs even more time. To accomplish this, you must have a skilled therapist and also commitment and determination.

Perhaps the most common cause for a setback in therapy is resistance. You may be ambivalent about whether you need therapy or whether it will help you. Resistance also happens when the subject turns uncomfortable—when therapy uncovers issues that make you feel threatened. As it happens, these issues are probably the ones you most need to work on. For example, if anger issues arise, you might feel you are being attacked or asked to let go of something that feels vital to you. This can bring therapy to a grinding halt.

Unfortunately, stigma regarding therapy is still widespread. You may fear what will happen if your friends and neighbors find out you're in therapy. You might not even want to be seen going into a therapist's office. Fear of being thought "crazy" can be a powerful deterrent. Because of images and stories in the news and entertainment media, there is an association between psychological issues and violence. This deters many people from getting help because they fear being labeled. Lots of jokes and insensitive speech trouble people who need help because that kind of talk reinforces the idea that psychological difficulty is something to be laughed at.

Sometimes, you may feel anxious that some of what you tell your therapist might become public knowledge. The feeling is real, but it's extremely unlikely to be true. Your therapist is forbidden to discuss your sessions with anyone else, even your family members, unless you give your permission. The only exception is that your therapist may discuss your treatment plan with their supervisor or a psychiatrist who may be able to prescribe medication. But those are rare occurrences. What you say in your sessions stays between you and your therapist.

Along those same lines is the issue of trust. You might be reluctant to tell your therapist about actions or issues that you find embarrassing. You could be afraid that they will be shocked, or worse—laugh. Rest assured that your therapist has heard it all. They are trained to accept what their clients tell them without shaming them for what they're feeling or what they've done. Even if your therapy moves into uncomfortable areas such as your sexual behavior (which it might not ever do), your therapist will not make fun of or blame you. An untrustworthy therapist will not last long in practice.

Your culture may also prevent you from either going to therapy or buying into the process. In Australia, for example, people are used to being on their own and denying that they need help. Other cultures where men and women are expected to be strong and silent can keep them from entering therapy. Even your own family may have an aversion to seeing a relative go into therapy for fear that they will be seen as the "bad guys" or that they will be required to go to therapy, too. They may try to talk you out of it or tell you that you don't need it.

Another of the most common setbacks in therapy is that you feel that the progress you're making is too slow. Therapy isn't like getting one shot of an antibiotic that will cure you. It does take some time and hard work on your part as well as your therapist's. But even though, in the past, psychoanalysis could take years and make no apparent progress, today's therapeutic methods emphasize shorter-term treatments so you can get back to your life. Sometimes, therapy can last as little as six weeks.

It can cause a setback in therapy if you have unrealistic treatment goals or goals that clash with your therapist's. For example, if you've suffered financial hardship, you may have the goal of gaining enough confidence to apply for another job, while your therapist might think it's important to explore and treat the depression you've been feeling or your underlying feelings of worthlessness. Of course, therapy can address all those issues, but usually not all at once. Your therapist may agree that building your confidence is necessary but that it won't be effective unless you work on the other issues as well.

Your healing process might also stall because you and your therapist have personalities that simply clash. It's best if you can get past this by honestly telling them how you feel. But if you simply don't click, it may be best to get a different therapist rather than continue without making progress. Of course, if your lack of progress is due to resistance (see above), a different therapist won't help. It's also best to be honest with yourself.

It's a big setback in your therapy if you have a new crisis or a relapse. Your therapist can handle it, but you may be distraught about it. It will seem like you're back to square one. In reality, the therapy you've already done can help you deal with the new setback. Your therapist can coach you through it. If you've already made progress, you can build on that. Don't give up! Therapy still has much to offer you.

If you experience any of these setbacks, you need to remember to be kind to yourself. Ask questions of your therapist regarding your mental health and well-being when you need to. Don't hold back, even if your emotions tell you that a subject is too painful to bring up. Above all, be your own best friend.

Be Your Own Best Friend

What does it mean to be your own best friend? It means that you should treat yourself with the caring and understanding that you would offer to a friend of yours who is experiencing pain and grief. If your friend was grieving, you would do whatever it took to comfort them. If they needed to be alone for a while, you would give them space. If they needed to be with someone who wouldn't pester them with unwanted advice, you would be a quiet, soothing presence for them. If they needed to talk, you'd listen to their feelings. If they wanted advice, you would do the best you could to offer it. If they wanted distraction, you'd take them out for coffee or a movie. If they needed physical comfort, you'd hug them.

Do the same for yourself. Reach out to others if that's what you need. Spend time by yourself if you need to be alone. Go for a walk in the woods if that's something that brings you comfort and healing. Invite someone to go for coffee with you if you need company or accept an invitation if they reach out to you. Ask them for recommendations if you need a therapist. Talk about your feelings if you trust a friend or family member who offers to listen. In other words, go after what you need and accept any help that's offered if you're ready to.

That's the secret to self-compassion *and* to being your own best friend: treating yourself as you would any other person you care for. You do this by cutting yourself some slack. You're facing challenges in your life right now. Accept that fact and your emotions about it. Do what you need to do to get by but don't lose hope.

Hope is one of the strongest forces that can work in your life. It has real power, and you should take advantage of that. Of course, that doesn't mean you should abandon the other strategies, such as therapy, mindfulness, and journaling, that you're practicing. Just remember that you have worth and deserve to treat yourself gently.

I discussed self-talk in Chapter 8, but I'm going to encourage you again to pay attention to it. Pay attention to the messages you send yourself—the thoughts and beliefs that you hold about yourself, your place in the world, and your actions. If you find that you're always criticizing yourself and describing yourself in unflattering terms, do your best to stop these thoughts and replace them with more accurate and positive thoughts about yourself. Use affirmations to reinforce positive qualities you have and good actions you've taken. If this is difficult for you, keep trying. You may have been hearing negative messages all your life. Replacing them with kindness and accurate perceptions may take some doing.

Self-care is a buzzword these days. Many people believe that it means shopping expeditions, spa treatments, bubble baths, and indulgent desserts. But the essence of self-care is doing things for yourself that feed your soul. The emphasis should be on actions that make you feel relaxed, centered, and calm. Of course, if that does mean spa treatments, it's fine. But consider other actions. Anything you do that promotes your well-being—physical, mental, and emotional—is a part of self-care. That includes eating properly, getting good sleep, and exercising. But it may also include playing music that you love, taking care of a pet, wearing comfortable clothing, or reviewing a photo album.

If you find there's too much pressure and too many demands on you, setting boundaries may help. You set time boundaries by deciding what you are willing and not willing to do. If someone tries to violate that boundary by asking you to do something or assumes that you will do it when you don't want to, simply say no. You'll be protecting your time, energy, and even your important relationships. By setting boundaries and maintaining them, you respect your own well-being and needs. You may find yourself feeling guilty about setting and enforcing boundaries but keep at it until it feels natural. While you're at it, try to break yourself out of the habit of explaining why when you say no to someone who's imposing on your time.

Forgiveness can be important, too—especially forgiving yourself. Forgiving other people who may have wronged you can bring you peace. But forgiving yourself does even more. Everyone makes mistakes. It's important to recognize them and admit to yourself that you may have done or said something you shouldn't have. But forgiving yourself lets you move past the self-blame that you've been beating yourself up with and move forward with better intentions. You can learn from your mistakes and treat them as opportunities for change and growth.

You can also be your own best friend by recognizing and celebrating your achievements. The progress you make in therapy is certainly worth celebrating. Meeting goals such as carrying through with an exercise program or maintaining a healthy diet are also accomplishments worthy of recognition. Take a moment to pat yourself on the back. You'd congratulate a friend who accomplished a goal, so do the same for yourself!

It may sound paradoxical, but positive relationships are also signs of being your own best friend. The people you associate with can add to your well-being. Being brave enough to reach out to other people can be as important as accepting friendship when someone else reaches out to you. Choosing people to surround yourself with who uplift you and nurture your spirit provides an environment in which your spirit can grow. You have the ability to be your own best friend!

Social Support

Other people can also be important when you're trying to recover from grief. You may have shied away from social interaction while you've been grieving, especially if you have suffered from depression. But getting back into the swing of things when you're ready can have positive effects on your emotions and mood.

First of all, when you have social interactions, your brain will release neurotransmitters like serotonin, dopamine, and oxytocin. All of them have a part to play in regulating your moods, but oxytocin is particularly important. It's often called the "bonding hormone," and it strengthens your attachment to other people, especially friends and family. It will make your social connections stronger.

Support from friends and family is something that can help you throughout the grieving process, but it will be especially important when you feel you are able to re-enter society, even in a small way. Social support is also known to reduce stress. Your family members and friends can go with you when you attend an event and drive you home if you realize you're not quite ready for that much interaction.

While talking to a mental health professional is best, talking with the members of your social support network can help as well. People who know you well can offer sympathy, a listening ear, and even a shoulder to cry on if you need it.

People who demonstrate empathy with your situation make it safe for you to express emotions. For example, you may feel that your coworkers simply don't understand what you've gone through. A friend who's been close to you while you were on your grief journey, on the other hand, can have a positive effect on your emotional regulation and even physical well-being. The social isolation that you've felt while grieving may have activated parts of your brain that regulate pain perception, including emotional pain. You can reverse this trend when you feel ready to try having some social interactions.

I've talked about the ways that grief can negatively affect your cognitive functions and memory. Being out among other people can help you regain your brain functions in these areas. Neuroplasticity, the brain's ability to reorganize itself, is enhanced by social support. These adaptive changes in the brain also support resilience and emotional regulation.

You've probably been feeling a lack of belonging because you've felt that no one understands what you've been going through. That's only natural. However, the positive effects of social interaction can create a feedback loop that enhances your social connections and all the positive benefits they bring. Sharing positive memories with friends and family members adds to the emotional associations in your brain and lessens the impact of the painful feelings of loss you've been experiencing.

Transforming Your Life

There are several different kinds of mindset, but only two of them will be useful as you try to transform your life after experiencing grief.

The one that's not helpful is one that many people have: the fixed mindset. This means that a person believes everything is set and settled the way it is. The world is cruel. Once you have experienced trauma, you will never be free of it. There's no way to change the way you think and feel. Your grief will go on and on.

That's simply not true. What is there that can counteract that kind of thinking? One thing is the growth mindset. It says that you believe you are capable of change. You can change the way you think about your grief. You can change how you cope with grief. You can change your outlook on life.

This isn't some kind of "Don't worry. Be happy" or "Good things will come to you if you think good thoughts" kind of magical thinking. You may think this goes against what I said about affirmations being helpful. But affirmations take a while to work. Repetition is necessary to change your thinking and improve your life through affirming statements. Quick, easy answers are not likely to be effective. Getting past grief takes work.

A growth mindset says that both the world and you are not fixed qualities. The world can change and so can your perception of it. You want to improve how you feel and how you think, especially about the situations that have brought you grief.

A transformation mindset is the third kind of way in which you can think. With a transformation mindset, you believe not just that the world can change but that you can also change. You realize that change is inevitable, and you can move along with it.

Life changed for you when you experienced a traumatic situation or major life event. It can and will change again. With a transformational mindset, you can help direct that change. You need to have confidence in your ability to create change and respond to the way that the world changes. You may have had setbacks, but you can grow and move on.

Change happens when you alter your life circumstances. For example, when you change your physical reality by taking up an exercise program, it will have an effect on not just your body but also your mind. You will begin to notice changes in the way you feel—less anxious and more centered. If you think you *should* feel a certain way in your reaction to grief, you can transform this into a different, more helpful kind of *should*: I should do the things that will bring me closer to a normal life and healing. I should work with my therapist. I should practice controlled breathing and mindfulness. Those are things that will help transform your life.

You're no longer at the mercy of the forces that surround you. You may not be able to change your circumstances, but you *can* change your emotions, feelings, and thoughts. And that will put you on the path to a new, better life. You change yourself by allowing yourself to change.

Moving Forward

If you find yourself asking how you will approach the future, you already have the answers. How you do this is no secret. You just have to look at your future with fresh eyes. To get a clearer view of the way forward, take the time to consider your past life. What have been your guiding principles? Have these changed at all during your journey through grief, or have you found that they have shifted? Perhaps your inner desire used to be to accumulate wealth, but once your material goods were gone, you have been able to see that other priorities such as kindness and service to others are equally important. Your grief has changed you in preparation for the rest of your life. You may have to rethink your life goals, your relationships, and your priorities in order to move forward.

When you were in the first stages of grief, you may have been plagued with depression. Now, you're ready for what's called "behavioral activation." It's the process by which you begin to engage again with the things you used to enjoy. The more you engage with life, the more you will be able to regain a new normal. Of course, it won't be the same normal that you experienced before grief overwhelmed you. You begin to achieve behavioral activation when you choose small activities and consciously plan to resume them.

You may have abandoned these activities because they no longer seemed important, you felt that you didn't have time for them, they took too much effort, or you simply no longer found them fun.

Perhaps they remind you of the way your life used to be before trauma came crashing down on you.

But taking up these activities again or discovering new ones will help you feel better, even if only a little bit. But recognize that that's progress. You're taking activities that will help you resolve your grief and implementing them. Sometimes, they're significant because they address the root causes of your grief. Other times, they heal you by getting you back in touch with people you've been avoiding when they could really have proved to be supportive.

Your new normal is very much a place of healing. It won't happen all at once, of course. Each little part of your life that you take back means chipping away at grief and depression. Your depression will fade to a manageable level, and your grief, while not entirely wiped out, will be manageable and livable.

One way you can begin to approach your new normal is to look at what has been taking up your time daily. What activities are directly related to your loss? Which ones cause you to worry, overthink, or feel drained? Which activities cause you anxiety? Do you feel that your days are too jam-packed, or do they feel largely empty?

It's time to rethink your daily schedule. If it's overly full of activities that keep you in a state of depression and inactivity, prune them. If you find activities that seem to reanimate your spark, devote more time to them. Finally, look at activities that will be therapeutic. Plug them into your schedule in the places where problems formerly lurked.

Moving forward involves rediscovering your passions. If you spent a certain amount of time each month working with charities that helped the poor and then became poor yourself and in need of help, you can renew your commitment to the food bank or outreach to the homeless. If you had a deep-seated desire to create beauty but your changed circumstances didn't allow you time to do so, renew your love of creative pursuits, whether they be painting, gardening, or singing in the church choir.

Making these changes, however, will probably require you to take small, gradual steps. Don't think that you have to change everything all at once. Move back into your life a little bit at a time. Realistic goals that you can fulfill will lead you to a sense of accomplishment. Congratulate yourself on the progress you make, however small it may seem. Making a difference starts with trying.

You've been through a time of upheaval. Regulating your life is one way to begin working through the pain. Developing a schedule for yourself and sticking to it will help you return to normalcy. Having a regular sleep time, diet, and exercise routine will provide a foundation for progress. Cultivate a sense of order. It will help you negotiate the path that lies before you. When your days or weeks are more predictable, you can leave behind the chaos that you've been experiencing.

Chapter 10:
Redefined Mind—New Life Dawns

It is during our darkest moments that we must focus to see the light. –Aristotle

In This Chapter

Relatively simple life lessons can successfully help you overcome serious life issues. You have gained emotional awareness and challenged adverse thoughts and belief systems. Allow these strategies and techniques that you've learned and the knowledge you've gained during this entire journey of healing to be the dawn of a new, better life. This is emotional growth. You have so much to be proud of!

Your Redefined Mind

You, the reader, are to be congratulated for taking the first step toward changing your life to something better. That first, most important step was realizing that you had a problem. You may have been fully aware of the concrete problems you had, such as financial hardship or a messy divorce. But your problems went far beyond that. You have had emotional difficulties as well, such as anxiety and depression. All of these issues have occupied your mind and caused emotional confusion. Once you recognized your problems, you were motivated to change your life for the better by working on your difficulties and finding solutions for them.

Now, you've learned that your emotional awareness will guide you to understand your challenges more completely. Of course, there are physical solutions to some of your problems—finding a new source of income if you're suffering from financial hardship, for example. But the real changes have happened in your emotions, thoughts, and feelings. Financial hardship, as you now know, also brings up negative emotions like despair, frustration, and helplessness, as well as depression and anxiety.

You've also committed to recovery and rebuilding your life. You've navigated through difficult and even dangerous parts of your life and your mental and emotional health. You've come from a dark place into the light of possibilities and changes.

Learning these truths has not been as simple as it sounds. Some people live with their difficulties and their negative emotions for years, suffering all the while. They may have found their circumstances too painful to face. They may have shielded themselves from the reality that is affecting them or chosen a form of self-preservation where natural grief is repressed. They may have recognized the major life issues and troubled emotions that affected them so strongly, but they have been unable to face them and try to resolve them.

Whatever the reasons for this suppression of emotions, admitting to experiencing and acknowledging them has prepared you for taking the next step. Now that you've realized that you have a problem and admitted the grief you've been hiding from, you're ready to take the second step toward healing—committing to the work of positive change.

The Story of Your Life

Your grief has changed the narrative of your life. How you view that narrative will change the rest of your life. Where you once felt whole and well, you've gone through great changes in circumstances, mood, and thought processes.

The changes in your circumstances have been profound. You may have experienced separation from loved ones, from your financial stability, and from your hopes and dreams. Now, you are working hard to renew those aspects of life and getting stronger every day. Even if you experience setbacks, you have the tools to cope. Your resilience and growth are now important parts of your story.

You've learned that grief has transformative power. You've been transformed in terms of how you view your life and how you've integrated your experiences into it. That doesn't mean you'll forget the past. But it's only one part of your story. Your new story is one of resilience. You've been through the storm and come out stronger and more centered, and you've proved to yourself that you can cope with adversity and sorrow.

Each step that you have taken on your journey has brought you to a new life. You can look back on what you've been through and feel pride at how far you've come. Instead of living with the wounds of grief, you've achieved true healing. You now have opportunities to contribute to the newly remade world you inhabit.

Your journey through grief has also been one of self-discovery. Every day, you can add to the chapters of your life with new scenes that express who you were meant to be and how far you've come. Your new life rises above grief, and you can begin to explore what's possible. You can embrace the changes that have happened in your life and the path that lies ahead.

Every day you live without being overwhelmed by grief is a testament to your resilience. You have taken the opportunity to renew your life, rewrite the story of that life, and begin new chapters that will take you into a new future—one that you live not on your knees, defeated, but one in which you can and will stand tall.

Your New Life

The truly important, hard work has begun. You've looked deep into yourself to conduct a self-analysis. You've recognized distortions in your thoughts and belief systems. You've challenged that inner voice that sends you harmful messages and impedes your growth. By working through the grieving process, you've prepared yourself for positive change and achieved rationality. Of course, this will also be quite difficult, but you're well prepared for it.

Positive change enriches you. The momentum you experience from it gives you even more momentum. Relief and the feeling of hope that the process creates in you give you a willingness and an ability to continue changing and growing. You'll be energized and invested in doing what you need to do to continue your recovery. Your enthusiasm will naturally grow.

Even though it's been difficult addressing your major life issues and confronting your grief, you've learned that you can find help as well. You now know that a trained, professional mental health counselor can help you with the process. You don't have to go it alone. They can not only help you gain control of your emotions once again, but they can also help you develop new coping skills that will prevent you from falling back into the dark place of your emotions when you encounter adversity in the future.

Throughout the process, you've been working on your brain and your mind. You've learned that you can retrain and reprogram the awesome computer that is your brain. In fact, it's just had an upgrade! You can change how your mind works with new ways of thinking and feeling. In addition to changing the way your computer processes your life, you've opened up new opportunities for yourself. You have enhanced emotional awareness as well as a new knowledge base. Your future is full of new opportunities thanks to what you've learned.

Many people who have been through these changes find themselves feeling like a new person—like they've been reborn. You may experience this feeling, too. When you feel this way, it's a sign of your determination not to slip back into a dysfunctional life of irrationality and grief.

You've done it! Welcome to the world of a redefined mind and a new life.

Conquering Adversity

Of course, there's no guarantee that you'll never encounter adversity again. Life holds surprises, and not all of them are good ones. Adversity comes to everyone, and, no doubt, you'll experience grief again. Your life can still feel precarious and difficult to negotiate. After all, you and your life aren't bulletproof!

At some point, you may have another cause for grief. You could experience an unexpected financial reversal. An intense relationship might end badly. Perhaps you'll be confronted by the death of a loved one or another major life issue such as the loss of a job, the death of a beloved pet, empty-nest syndrome, or failure in school. Even the recent COVID-19 pandemic was a cause for grief when people were faced with isolation, loneliness, the inability to attend family or religious celebrations, and fear of illness. You'll naturally feel all the emotions associated with that difficulty. Grief will reappear in all its rawness.

However, this time, you'll be better prepared to deal with it. You'll have better emotional perceptions and a better perspective on what is occurring in your life. You've been there before and were able to work through the situation to a more positive resolution. Even though you'll experience grief, heartache, sorrow, regret, and all the emotions that adversity brings, you have the tools to triumph. This time, you won't allow yourself to be controlled by those emotions. You'll feel them, but you won't let them take over your life.

Relish the Freedom

Freedom is an amazing feeling and something that we're always desiring, chasing, and grasping at. Sometimes it seems impossibly far away, and at other times, it's right next door or even closer. We envy those who seem to have it. But we never really know.

Someone who seems to have it all may have freedom from material hardship, but they can still lack freedom when it comes to family matters or the possibility of illness. They can experience a loss of freedom when a tragedy strikes, and grief takes over their life. While we often think that wealth brings freedom, it doesn't always. Even someone who is rich in every material way may not be free from loneliness, sadness, or a feeling of emptiness. And they may lack the emotional awareness to realize their problem or the skills to free themselves from its grasp.

You're looking at a new kind of freedom—freedom to experience life in all its variety, to negotiate the rough patches, and to come out the other side even stronger. When you have negative or distorted thoughts, you'll be able to develop positive alternatives to replace them. This is true emotional growth.

Freedom from hardship is an impossible goal. None of us knows what the future will bring. But you can experience freedom from the aftermath of adversity. When freedom appears, relish it! But never forget that you have the tools to create that freedom and to find it again, even when you think you've lost it.

Emotional strength and freedom are within your power!

Conclusion

A man watches his pear tree day after day, impatient for the ripening of the fruit. Let him attempt to force the process, and he may spoil both fruit and tree. But let him patiently wait, and the ripe pear at length falls into his lap. –Abraham Lincoln

Over the past two decades, I have counseled many people in a nonclinical setting, using the techniques and insights I've shared with you in this book. I hope you have found the content to be relatable and understandable. If it is, I've done my job!

To me, professional counseling is a great privilege. Being able to help others through their grief, anxiety, and depression is a wondrous thing. When someone with so much pain invites me into their life, I feel that I can truly help. The people I counsel need me to address serious issues because they simply cannot do it themselves. They invite me into their lives and share their pain with me. In turn, I get to help them put their lives back together.

This book is for you if you are trying to deal with grief from a major life event. The topics I chose are areas I have encountered in my counseling practice. Much of the advice you'll find in other books about grief focuses on grief caused by the death of a loved one. But there are many other causes of grief. You may have experienced different sorts of loss—the loss of a relationship through separation or divorce, a financial reversal, or the loss of a job or a friend, to name a few. Whatever the cause, grief affects you in predictable ways.

Everyone experiences grief in different and very personal ways. How you react has been influenced by personal factors such as your support system, your culture and heritage, your emotional style, and your coping skills. Your experience of grief is unique, but at the same time you share certain universal feelings. Your grief may not have followed the exact five stages of the grief model that so many people talk about.

Your grief journey may have taken a different path. I hope you have come to realize that your personal grief journey is a valid one.

If you have an honest approach and clear understanding, you can achieve positive thoughts and behavior. It can be exhilarating when disturbing emotions no longer control your life!

To help you through your grief, I've introduced you to the ways the awesome human brain—your own personal supercomputer—works. The neurons, synapses, neurotransmitters, and brain structures combine to create your emotions, thoughts, and feelings. In turn, those emotions, thoughts, and feelings combine to determine your behavior.

Your brain and mind are intimately involved in how you process grief. Your emotions, thoughts, and feelings work together to create your response. Your body is involved as well. Neurotransmitters and hormones that the brain regulates affect your heart rate, respiration, pain levels, and more. If you experience depression and anxiety, you may also encounter physical symptoms like migraines, difficulty sleeping, and heart trouble. Additionally, emotional reactions such as irritability, loneliness, or loss of interest in previously enjoyed activities can occur.

Grief can lead to anxiety and depression. These are serious conditions that can incapacitate you when it comes to daily functioning. You may not be able to get to sleep, or you may not be able to get out of bed in the morning. You could be unable to keep up with your daily chores and regular activities. You might avoid all human contact.

Anxiety and depression have physical effects as well. Some can be deadly. Problems with your blood pressure and heart rate can indicate disorders that, if they continue, can be life-threatening. Other effects can be debilitating—migraines, muscle tension, and gastrointestinal symptoms, among others. Anxiety and depression can send you into a spiral. The physical symptoms can make you even more anxious and depressed.

Most people think of grief as being caused by the death of a friend or loved one. That can certainly be true, and I covered those traumatic events in Book 1 of this series. However, other circumstances can leave you with grief. Divorce, separation, or estrangement are among them. The same principles you've learned in this book will apply to those situations as well. Many other adverse life events will involve a grieving process. I'll address them in the third book of this series.

When you divorce, you lose a loved one or someone whom you once loved. You can experience grief over the fact that you are parting or over the fact that you gave your love to someone who was not worthy of it. You may grieve over the necessity of removing this person from your life. Even if the divorce is amicable, you may still grieve the fact that the relationship is over or the fact that the good times together will never come again.

If you have children, you could be grieving that your family is no longer united. You may also be forced into a different standard of living and feel grief at the loss of the life you have known. The uncertainty you face can send you into depression and anxiety. If your identity was bound up in being part of a couple, losing that may leave you grieving the fact that your whole identity is changing.

Estrangement from your children is also possible in a divorce situation. This wrenching development is often a cause for anxiety, depression, and grief. Your bond with your child or children is severed, and it may never be healed. You may fear that your ex-partner will cause or deepen the estrangement by how they speak of you to the children. Or you may experience grief at the loss of your connection with them and the thought that you will not be a part of their lives anymore, or at least not a big part. You may grieve missing out on the special occasions in their lives, such as graduation, marriage, and the birth of grandchildren.

You can be estranged from close friends, too. You may at first think that you've had some kind of misunderstanding, but sometimes the breach is irreparable. You may think at first that the connection will be restored somehow, but when it isn't, you can suffer anxiety, depression, and grief. It changes your social connections and leaves a gap in your life. The ending of that relationship can leave you emotionally distraught, wishing that the connection could be rekindled. It leaves your life with a hole in it, and you will grieve the loss of someone you have shared special moments, good times, and even confidences with.

If your circle of friends has been limited, the loss of even one of them can be extremely painful. Any loss like that may result in grief.

Yet another cause for grief is financial hardship, especially if it results in poverty. The losses you suffer may include a loss of identity, dignity, security, social position, and connections or opportunities. You may develop a fear of losing what you have left. You may be unable to meet your own or your family's basic needs. Financial hardship and poverty can have a detrimental effect on your mental health, too, leaving you at risk for anxiety, depression, and grief. You can feel shame and powerlessness, and even social stigma and isolation. You can also feel grief regarding the impact your poverty will have on your family relationships, especially those with your children.

Fortunately, there are ways to address grief from any of these causes. You don't have to go through the effects by yourself. You can find help from a mental health professional such as a psychiatrist, psychologist, counselor, or therapist. I've seen and personally experienced how reaching out to one of these practitioners can help you understand your situation and rebuild your life.

A therapist can use techniques such as CBT, ACT, or other forms of talk therapy. They can recommend practices such as controlled breathing, mindfulness, affirmations, and journaling that you can do on your own. If necessary, a mental health professional can even prescribe antidepressants or anti-anxiety medications that can get you through depression and anxiety until the time when you're able to address and work on the root causes of your grief.

Those root causes may not be obvious at first. Of course, if you've just been through an event like a messy divorce, that will be the primary cause of your grief. But it's also possible that deeper causes lie hidden in your childhood, for example. If you didn't get the love and support you needed from your family back then, the grief over that lack may complicate your current feelings of grief. Or if you've suffered from financial hardship recently, your reaction may be complicated by a period during your growing-up years when your needs and wants were not met because of a lack of funds.

Social support can also help you when you are troubled by grief of any type. You may have close friends who have also been through traumatic grief, and talking with them is a good idea. There are also grief support groups online and in person. Your doctor or mental health professional can put you in touch with a support group or therapy group in your area. Building or rebuilding your support system can be a vital step in transitioning into your new life.

This book has presented you with ways to cope with grief and come through to the other side renewed in spirit. You've discovered ways to be your own best friend and to give yourself the tools you need to defeat the grief that threatened to take over your life. Your process of handling grief has enabled you to move forward with your life and rebuild what you've lost, whether that is your stability, your peace of mind, or your relationships. In a very real sense, your grief journey from despair to healing has transformed your life. Your new normal may not look exactly like the one that you imagined, but you will be stronger and better able to get on with your newly rediscovered life.

Grief is dark—but it can lighten. Now there is hope for you to live life fully again!

The third book in this series will deal with grief caused by other extremely tragic events, the kind that can lead to "prolonged grief" or "complicated grief." You'll find the same kinds of help and hope in there that you've found in the first two volumes. Thank you for letting me join you on your journey!

Book Review

Dear Reader, it has been my privilege to walk with you and guide you at this difficult time.

I trust I was able to show how there can be peace in your life again.

If you found solace in my book, I will be forever grateful if you could leave me a Review.

A moment of your time can encourage more people to benefit from this content.

The QR codes below will direct you to the Review Page or Home Page of this book in your country/marketplace. You can find "Customer Reviews" or "Review this product" on the left-hand side of the Book's Homepage. Your feedback is greatly appreciated.

Thank you.

USA

UK

Canada

Australia

References

Ackerman, C. (2017, June 18). *19 narrative therapy techniques, interventions & worksheets*. Positive Psychology. https://positivepsychology.com/narrative-therapy

American Psychological Association. (2022). *Anxiety*. https://www.apa.org/topics/anxiety

Anxiety and Depression Association of America. (022, October 28). *Facts & statistics*. ADAA. https://adaa.org/understanding-anxiety/facts-statistics

Anxiety and Depression Association of America. (n.d.). *What is depression?* ADAA. https://adaa.org/understanding-anxiety/depression

Chand, S. P., Kuckel, D. P., & Huecker, M. R. (2022). Cognitive behavior therapy. In *StatPearls*. StatPearls Publishing.

Cherney, K. (2022, September 19). *Effects of anxiety on the body*. Healthline. https://www.healthline.com/health/anxiety/effects-on-body#how-does-it-feel

Cleveland Clinic. (2023, January 13). *Depression symptoms, causes, & treatment*. https://my.clevelandclinic.org/health/diseases/9290-depression

Fields, L. (2021, March 14). *Is it the "baby blues" or postpartum depression?* WebMD. https://www.webmd.com/depression/postpartum-depression/postpartum-depression-baby-blues

Gautama Buddha. (n.d.). *A quote by Gautama Buddha*. (n.d.). Goodreads. https://www.goodreads.com/quotes/7156663-your-worst-enemy-cannot-hurt-you-as-much-as-your

Greater Good in Action. (n.d.). *Body scan meditation*. Berkeley University of California. https://ggia.berkeley.edu/practice/body_scan_meditation

Hairston, S. (2022, March 2). *5 ways to get better results in therapy (The tips we use)*. OpenCounseling. https://blog.opencounseling.com/relationship-with-your-therapist/

Haley, E. (2016, March 31). *Reconnecting with life after loss (One step at a time)*. What's Your Grief. https://whatsyourgrief.com/reconnecting-with-life-after-loss/

Hamilton, D. (2022, January 27). *The science of affirmations*. David R Hamilton. https://drdavidhamilton.com/the-science-of-affirmations/

Henry Ford Health Staff. (2018). *How coping with grief can affect your brain*. Henry Ford. https://www.henryford.com/blog/2018/06/how-coping-with-grief-can-affect-your-brain

Hock, R. S., Or, F., Kolappa, K., Burkey, M. D., Surkan, P. J., & Eaton, W. W. (2012). A new resolution for global mental health. *Lancet*, *379*(9824), 1367–1368. https://doi.org/10.1016/S0140-6736(12)60243-8

Humana. (n.d.). *Screening your patients for loneliness*. Aging Idaho. https://aging.idaho.gov/wp-content/uploads/2020/05/Loneliness_Physician_Quick_Guide_5.7.2020.pdf

Joseph Rowntree Foundation. (2023, January 20). *Overall U.K. poverty rates*. https://www.jrf.org.uk/data/overall-uk-poverty-rates

Kelly, L. (2021, September 23). *7 effective grief therapy techniques*. Talkspace. https://www.talkspace.com/blog/grief-therapy-techniques/

King, B. J. (n.d.). *A quote by Billie Jean King*. Goodreads. https://www.goodreads.com/author/quotes/74527.Billie_Jean_King

Lee, E. (2021, May 17). *12 of Prince Harry's most candid quotes about mental health*. IHeart. https://www.iheart.com/content/2021-05-17-12-of-prince-harrys-most-candid-quotes-about-mental-health

Mandela, N. (n.d.). *Nelson Mandela quote*. Quotery. https://www.quotery.com/quotes/greatest-glory-living-lies-not

McLeod, S. (2018). *Maslow's hierarchy of needs*. Simply Psychology. https://canadacollege.edu/dreamers/docs/Maslows-Hierarchy-of-Needs.pdf

Millman, D. (n.d.). *A quote by Dan Millman*. Goodreads. https://www.goodreads.com/quotes/10158365-you-don-t-have-to-control-your-thoughts-you-just-have

Moberly, N. (2021, October 21). *How to process grief and find healthy ways to overcome loss*. BetterUp. https://www.betterup.com/blog/how-to-process-grief

Moore, M. (2022, September 21). *CBT vs. DBT: What's the difference?* PsychCentral. https://psychcentral.com/lib/whats-the-difference-between-cbt-and-dbt#main-differences

National Institutes of Neurological Disorders and Stroke. (n.d.). *Brain basics: Know your brain*. National Institutes of Health. https://www.ninds.nih.gov/health-information/public-education/brain-basics/brain-basics-know-your-brain

News in Health. (2021, June 1). *Mindfulness for your health*. National Institutes of Health. https://newsinhealth.nih.gov/2021/06/mindfulness-your-health

Ney, J. (2023, October 4). *The surprising poverty levels across the U.S*. Time. https://time.com/6320076/american-poverty-levels-state-by-state/

Obama, B. (n.d.). *Barack Obama quote*. Quote Catalog. https://quotecatalog.com/quote/barack-obama-to-anyone-out-t-Y7APqD1

Peer, A. (2018, November 21). *Global poverty: Facts, FAQs, and how to help*. World Vision. https://www.worldvision.org/sponsorship-news-stories/global-poverty-facts#facts

Piedmont. (n.d.) *10 fun facts about your brain*. https://www.piedmont.org/living-real-change/10-fun-facts-about-your-brain

Pilmeyer, J., Huijbers, W., Lamerichs, R., Jansen, J. F. A., Breeuwer, M., & Zinger, S. (2022). Functional MRI in major depressive disorder: A review of findings, limitations, and future prospects. *Journal of Neuroimaging, 32*(4), 582–595. https://doi.org/10.1111/jon.13011

Probasco, J. (2023, October 19). *Where to look for help from the government*. Investopedia. https://www.investopedia.com/government-assistance-programs-4845368

Psychology Today Staff. (2017). *Acceptance and commitment therapy*. Psychology Today. https://www.psychologytoday.com/us/therapy-types/acceptance-and-commitment-therapy

Psychology Today Staff. (2019). *Narrative therapy*. Psychology Today. https://www.psychologytoday.com/us/therapy-types/narrative-therapy

Rumi. (n.d.). *A quote by Rumi*. Goodreads. https://www.goodreads.com/quotes/551027-yesterday-i-was-clever-so-i-wanted-to-change-the

Ryan, P. (2019, April 29). *Pink opens up about therapy, miscarriage at 17: "You feel like your body is broken."* USA Today. https://www.usatoday.com/story/life/music/2019/04/29/pink-talks-therapy-miscarriages-you-feel-like-your-body-broken/3590509002/

Saumya. (2022, December 22). *What is the difference between brain and mind?* Jagran Josh. https://www.jagranjosh.com/general-knowledge/difference-between-brain-and-mind-1671691029-1

Seow, E. (2018, March 28). *Which one comes first, thoughts or emotions?* Medium. https://medium.com/undelusional/which-one-comes-first-thoughts-or-emotions-624ea127978e

Shah, M. (2022, July 13). *If you look at what you have in life, you'll always have more.* SetQuotes. https://www.setquotes.com/if-you-look-at-what-you-have-in-life-youll-always-have-more/

Shulman, L. (2021, September 29). *Healing your brain after loss: How grief rewires the brain.* American Brain Foundation. https://www.americanbrainfoundation.org/how-tragedy-affects-the-brain/

Sima, R. (2023, December 6). *In the mystery of postpartum depression, the immune system offers clues.* Washington Post. https://www.washingtonpost.com/wellness/2023/12/06/postpartum-depression-immune-system/

Tompa, R. (2022, February 14). *A map of all our brains' blood vessel cells finds new clues to Alzheimer's disease.* Allen Institute. https://alleninstitute.org/news/a-map-of-all-our-brains-blood-vessel-cells-finds-new-clues-to-alzheimers-disease/

Transformations Treatment Center. (n.d.). *Depression.* https://www.transformationstreatment.center/mental-health/depression

UNSW Sydney. (2022, October 14). *One in eight people in Australia is living in poverty, as cost of living pressures increase.* UNSW Newsroom. https://newsroom.unsw.edu.au/news/social-affairs/one-eight-people-australia-living-poverty-cost-living-pressures-increase

UWA. (2019, June 27). *Science of emotion: The basics of emotional psychology.* UWA Online. https://online.uwa.edu/news/emotional-psychology

Wilson, S., & Burford, M. (2021, October 23). *5 ways depression can physically affect the brain.* Healthline. https://www.healthline.com/health/depression-physical-effects-on-the-brain#effects-of-depression

Yale School of Medicine. (n.d.). *Overview.* https://medicine.yale.edu/lab/colon_ramos/overview

Zaccaro, A., Piarulli, A., Laurino, M., Garbella, E., Menicucci, D., Neri, B., & Gemignani, A. (2018). How breath-control can change your life: A systematic review on psycho-physiological correlates of slow breathing. *Frontiers in Human Neuroscience, 12*(353), 1–16. https://doi.org/10.3389/fnhum.2018.00353

Zhang, F.-F., Peng, W., Sweeney, J. A., Jia, Z.-Y., & Gong, Q.-Y. (2018). Brain structure alterations in depression: Psychoradiological evidence. *CNS Neuroscience & Therapeutics, 24*(11), 994–1003. https://doi.org/10.1111/cns.12835

www.ingramcontent.com/pod-product-compliance
Lightning Source LLC
Chambersburg PA
CBHW061656040426
42446CB00010B/1764